Carrie Grant MBE and **David Grant MBE** are BAFTA award-winning broadcasters, vocal coaches, leadership coaches and pastors. Their TV and music career has spanned more than 40 years, from numerous hit records to presenting BBC 1's *The One Show* and *Songs of Praise*. Their public speaking and preaching have taken them around the world, and for the past 12 years they have led a church in their home. They have been married for 34 years and have four children, all of whom have additional needs. They are passionate about diversity and inclusion.

FIRST 30 DAYS OF WALKING WITH JESUS

Your guide to understanding the
Christian life

Carrie and David Grant

First published in Great Britain in 2022

Society for Promoting Christian Knowledge
36 Causton Street
London SW1P 4ST
www.spck.org.uk

British Library Cataloguing-in-Publication Data
A catalogue record for this book is available from the British Library

ISBN 978-0-281-08678-8
eBook ISBN 978-0-281-08679-5

1 3 5 7 9 10 8 6 4 2

Typeset by Manila Typesetting Company
First printed in Great Britain by Clays Ltd, Elcograf S.p.A.

eBook by Manila Typesetting Company

Produced on paper from sustainable forests

To our four beautiful children –

who have taught us so much about walking with Jesus

Contents

Contents

Contents

Contributors

This book would not be what it is without the extraordinary friends who have helped with their contributions.

Lois Burgess Lois is an Assistant Headteacher for Inclusion in a large secondary school in a deprived area of London.

Andre Radmall Andre is a therapist and bestselling author.

Caleb Storkey Caleb is an award-winning author, speaker and entrepreneur.

Beth Vargeson Beth is a creative artist using her gifting to make spiritual and reflective art.

Mark Vargeson Mark is passionate about local government and leads a team in family services.

Foreword

In the late 1990s, Carrie and David arrived at our church with their family – they were simply wanting to worship and be closer to Jesus, and to find a place for their children to grow to know Jesus too. This book captures that longing – it's still burning in their hearts, not just for themselves and their family but for everyone who comes into their lives.

Since then, we have had the joy of helping them lead a church in their home. That is not a place where a leader can hide. We have watched them process their own past, their highs and lows, their health, their working lives and their family's life. Through it all they have known themselves loved and valued by God, they have clung to Jesus in worship and they have grounded their lives on the eternal truths of the Bible.

We have also watched them putting into practice, not just speaking about, God's radically inclusive grace and love as they have welcomed, with extravagant generosity, all whom God has brought to them. In the midst of highly pressured lives, both at work and at home, they find time for everyone, wherever they are on their spiritual journey. 'Doing life miles together,' is their maxim. The impact of this is that many have found faith in Jesus for the first time, some almost immediately and some after many years. Others have come back to faith in Jesus after time spent in the barren desert of disappointment and pain. And others have grown in their appreciation of what it means to be followers of Jesus in this broken, imperfect world.

This book is written with all those people in mind, reflecting what they have discovered to be some of the most essential truths for life. But it is especially foundational for those new to faith in Jesus.

Establishing these foundation stones, and the practice of meditating daily on Scripture, will help build a life that will stand through the storms that the twenty-first century will throw up.

Its pithy style reflects Carrie and David's experience as sought-after motivational speakers. And its occasionally poetic approach reflects their own creativity and thoughtfulness. You don't have to have church or previous religious experience to understand it. But, equally, if you read it slowly, you will discover there is so much to 'chew the cud' on.

Having journeyed with God for many years, Carrie and David recognize that the process of change is not always as fast as we might like: 'we grow and change gradually over time'. What they have really grasped, and long for others to grasp, is that the process happens 'from the inside out'. We have no hesitation in commending not just this book, but also this approach to the Bible, 'as we grow in recognizing and living in God's amazing love for us'.

John and Anne Coles

Day 1
Starting the journey

Every journey starts with a single step. Those who are searching for God start the journey or come to God or become aware of him in different places and at different paces. Some come crashing face to face; for others it's a slow burn, a gradual awakening, a dawning realization; for some it's as though God has always been there and one day we simply opened the door; for others still it's the deconstruction of a previous religious experience, 'Christian' or otherwise.

There's no right or wrong way to come to faith; each walk should be respected and accepted. One of the greatest gifts God gives us is choice. He will not push or force his way in. He simply knocks on the door of our lives and waits.

God is the big-picture King-of-the-Universe, but he is also deeply personal. He calls himself 'I am', which, translated from the Hebrew (the language of the Old Testament), could be better expressed in English as, 'I am who you need me to be, when you need me to be it.'

The Christian faith is often described as personal because it is characterized by relationship with him. God has had this 'personal' nature from the beginning of time. He created humans for relationship with him and with one another. He is present; he is personal – intimate, even. This intimacy is not for treats or special occasions; it is for all day, every day. God has perfect parental characteristics: love, truth, protection, patience, justice – he is the ultimate parent.

Out of this desire for relationship and reconciliation, God came as Jesus to the earth. Many people were awaiting a Messiah (meaning 'saviour') and had ideas about what he would be like. Some were expecting a mighty warrior-type king who would rescue them and win military battles for them, but God had other plans. Jesus would be born into a regular Jewish family in a regular place among regular people. Unfortunately, many couldn't recognize him for who he was. They couldn't see he was the King of the Universe because he went to the outcasts, the controversially marginalized, interacting, loving, healing, serving and saving them. He came for all people. His love and actions were scandalous to the religious leaders as, rather than obeying them, he corrected them, refusing to be contained by their rules. He put people first. It makes you wonder how he would be received today.

God is also spirit, and his Spirit lives in all people. When we say yes to God, we become super aware of the Holy Spirit living in us. The Spirit beckons us, guides us, directs us, tells us of God's love, saying, 'This is the truth. Walk this way.'

Revelation 3.20 (TPT)

Behold, I'm standing at the door, knocking. If your heart is open to hear my voice and you open the door *within*, I will come in to you and feast with you, and you will feast with me.

Day 2
Creation

Once there was nothing. No people. No planet. No universe. No coffee shops!

Then

Suddenly

There was life.

God did this. It wasn't an accident. How could something possibly come from nothing?

God breathed Spirit breath over the soup of emptiness, the inky blackness. He birthed life into the silent void.

Like a picture coming into focus, God developed this life into stars, planets and people. Genesis 1 is a poem that describes this process as taking six days. These were probably not days as we understand them (although some Christians think they were). What it was, though, was a *process*.

Creation is always a process. We are conceived in a second. We are carried for nine months. We are born and then grow over a lifetime. Creation never stops. Creation is not a one-off event. It never stops. To try to lock down life and stand against its unpredictable, out-of-control flow is to stand against the very fact of creation. To try to control creation by draining the resources of our planet rather than loving and caring for it is an exercise in self-destruction.

Science shows us that, since the start of time, the universe has been moving outward. Nothing is static. God is always moving out to embrace, love and connect. We can participate in this creativity in every area of our lives. Creativity is not just for the artists. It is hardwired into us by our creator God. To participate and appreciate creation is to see beyond the horizon to worlds as yet undiscovered.

Above all, thinking about creation reminds us that God was always there before us. Our very existence is rooted in his breath. *This* is our ultimate reality. It's easy to forget this when we are fighting the pressures of life. Paying bills, holding relationships together, loving kids who don't love back and fighting Instagram envy can pull us into inky blackness. Creation reminds us to lift our gaze to the distant horizon, where God is calling and the stars are shining in unknown galaxies.

Genesis 1.1–2 (MSG)

In the beginning

First this: God created the Heavens and Earth – all you see, all you don't see. Earth was a soup of nothingness, a bottomless emptiness, an inky blackness. God's Spirit brooded like a bird above the watery abyss.

Day 3
Saved

People who identify themselves as Christians or followers of Jesus will often say they have been 'saved', but what does this mean? Saved from what?

Saved from the tyranny of having to keep up with the world's expectations, or indeed saved from the demands of a religious construct? Saved from having to be something we are not; saved from our own harsh inner judge? Saved from being overpowered by addiction and meaningless or hurtful actions towards ourselves or others, this thing we call sin? Saved from hostility towards God? Saved from the power that our past pain uses to keep us in captivity? All these things are rotting death and darkness, ruling our lives until the day we die and it's finally over.

But what if . . . what if there was a way we could experience new life now – here, today, in all its fullness, no matter what our circumstances; a life that, once we drop the flesh, leads to eternal life where there will be no more death or mourning or crying or pain? Jesus tells us that all that rotting death and darkness was laid on him when he was crucified, and as a result we can enter into his life-giving and experience real freedom in this and in the next life. Two for the price of one! This 'salvation' is for our eternal existence and also for our life right now, here on earth.

Not only are we saved, past tense, but we are also being saved. It's an ongoing process as our relationship with God evolves and grows.

We access the relationship just as we are; we begin the journey where we are, whether that's on a mountaintop, having had a mind-blowing revelation of who God is, or a grudging acceptance that, like it or not, God is real and Jesus is exactly who he said he was.

C. S. Lewis, recounting his saving experience, said:

In the Trinity Term of 1929 I gave in, and admitted that God was God, and knelt and prayed: perhaps, that night, the most dejected and reluctant convert in all England. I did not then see what is now the most shining and obvious thing; the Divine humility which will accept a convert even on such terms.[1]

John 3.16–17

Born again

For God so loved the world that he gave his one and only Son, that whoever believes in him shall not perish but have eternal life. For God did not send his Son into the world to condemn the world, but to save the world through him.

Day 4

Trusting the Father

God's gift of eternal life is just that: a gift. We may question this: 'Isn't that a bit easy? Surely, I have to do something in return? Where's the invoice?'

This has been one of the stumbling blocks of the church throughout history – the juxtaposition between earning our salvation and being gifted our salvation. People can feel very unsafe with the concept that God just gives it away. It makes no sense; it's scandalous, irresponsible even.

Does God ask for nothing in return? No.

He doesn't ask for our good works and best behaviour; he asks for way more. He asks for our lives. He asks to be believed in. He asks us to trust him; he asks us to depend on him fully. He asks us to have faith in him. He wants relationship. On balance, a few good works and behavioural changes would be the easier option.

The Father knows us and wants to be known by us. Like all relationships in life, it takes time to grow. As we walk beside him, we learn that God loves us. He is full of compassion; he is faithful, good and reliable; he fights our battles, wants to heal our broken places and give us hope and purpose.

This concept of God can be hard to grasp if our experiences of being parented have been challenging. God is like no earthly father; neither is he a scary being waiting for the opportunity to punish us. This grumpy God is a church construct that has been used to keep people in line, to control them with guilt and to pull them into service. This is not the God of the Bible.

God wants us to be confident with him, like little children. He wants us to boldly ask for his help with expectation of a response.

He is a willing Father, a perfect Father, and we are safe with him. He is ready and waiting for us to walk with him and to allow him to lead us.

Matthew 11.27–30 (MSG)

The unforced rhythms of grace

Jesus resumed talking to the people, but now tenderly. 'The Father has given me all these things to do and say. This is a unique Father–Son operation, coming out of Father and Son intimacies and knowledge. No one knows the Son the way the Father does, nor the Father the way the Son does. But I'm not keeping it to myself; I'm ready to go over it line by line with anyone willing to listen.

'Are you tired? Worn out? Burned out on religion? Come to me. Get away with me and you'll recover your life. I'll show you how to take a real rest. Walk with me and work with me – watch how I do it. Learn the unforced rhythms of grace. I won't lay anything heavy or ill-fitting on you. Keep company with me and you'll learn to live freely and lightly.'

Day 5
What is Jesus like?

Good relationships are about two-way loving, two-way trust and truly knowing someone and being known.

Trust can take time.

We are taught – don't trust strangers. This is good advice.

Who is Jesus?

Jesus loved people; he hung out with the people no one else wanted to hang out with – the controversially marginalized. He gave value to women and children; he touched the untouchable and healed them. Every time religious people tried to catch him out, he came back at them with a profound statement that would turn everyone's thinking on its head. He brought people together, empowered them and gave them purpose.

His love allowed for difference, for character and personality to shine. He always valued the relationship over the rules: healing on the Jewish day of rest, not condemning people who were caught red-handed, letting the young gather to chew the cud with him. He loved the people, all people. He turned their world upside down, calling out hypocrisy and putting the heart back into the relationship.

From his life-giving manifesto spoken through the Sermon on the Mount to his upturning tables outside the temple; from his feeding the hungry and healing the sick to speaking in riddles that allowed people to explore their own journey; from speaking to thousands hanging on his every word to him staying silent in front of those who had the power to stop his death; from his intimate, insightful, one-to-one conversations to dying on the cross to save the world.

Good relationships involve surrender. Not a surrender that is commanded or covertly demanded. Jesus leads the way, saying, 'Me first,' then lays an invitation at our door.

No forcing. Free choice.

Luke 19.10

For the Son of Man came to seek and to save the lost.

Day 6
Communicating with God

Communication with God is a key element of growth in our understanding and relationship with God. We don't just hear from God through the Bible or the experiences of others; we can also have an ongoing, daily, personal interaction with him. So let's talk about prayer.

Prayer is often misunderstood. People often think of it as a fancy style of speech that must be learned and mastered, or they take the Lord's Prayer as something to be memorized and recited and think that's the sum total of prayer. In reality, prayer is communication, talking to God in your own style, whether it be out loud or quietly, happy or sad, with or without words. And it's also listening to and sensing God.

Prayer is not a one-way monologue, nor is it simply words of hope spoken out into a universal void. God hears and responds. As with any communication, it helps to know with whom you are talking. It's important to know that the person you're talking to loves you, approves of you, delights in you, and always longs to hear from and speak to you.

Sometimes we may find ourselves crying out to God for change or a breakthrough. God is not silent, but when we are experiencing trauma, it can often feel this way. To some, it feels as though God speaks all the way through the pain, and to others he appears to be saying nothing. He may not always answer at the time or in the way that we expect him to, but God responds nonetheless. He either changes the situation we are in or changes us in the situation – often both, so whichever way you look at it, prayer really does change things. God can move mountains and move in our lives in miraculous ways. Dare to ask him.

What does prayer look like?

It's your words, however clear or jumbled; it's your thoughts, however shaped or random; it's your groans and sighs, your hopes and dreams, your faith, your doubts and your fears. God hears and responds to them all. You can tell him your cares because he cares for you. Prayer is you being yourself with God, who went to extraordinary lengths to initiate the conversation because you mean more to him than you could ever know. Prayer is where you begin by knowing that whatever you say, feel or think, you will always be accepted and never rejected, and you have the security of knowing that, when there are no words to adequately express how you feel, God interprets that too.

Our reading today says, 'If we don't know how or what to pray, it doesn't matter. He does our praying in and for us, making prayer out of our wordless sighs, our aching groans.'

That's prayer. Welcome to the most intimate, confidential interaction of your life.

Romans 8.26 (MSG)

How to pray

If we don't know how or what to pray, it doesn't matter. He does our praying in and for us, making prayer out of our wordless sighs, our aching groans.

Day 7
Made in his image

The Bible tells us that we are made in God's image. This can be difficult to grasp if we don't like ourselves or if there are parts of ourselves we really battle with. God has made us just the way he intended – diverse; no mistakes. We are a reflection of him and we were made to know him. The more we know him, the more we reflect him.

Individual identities are created in the womb, then develop first through our culture and family and continue to evolve and change over time, depending on our life experiences, work, interests and the various relationships we have with the people around us. Identities are complex, made up of all the little things that make us unique (the 'I' each of us carries within), and change over time as we interact with and experience the world around us. However, in our imperfect world, identities are damaged and influenced by absorbing failure, loss or abuse. We live in a flawed world and yet we can be free to discover our true identity and purpose the more closely we are drawn to God. As the scripture says, 'It's in Christ that we find out who we are and what we are living for' (Eph. 1.11 MSG).

God doesn't make mistakes. We are all one-offs. We are unique, each different, each with our own ways, character, personality, look, style, gifts and talents. He wants us to be complete, just as he intended. There aren't particular Christians in the world who have a monopoly on the 'correct' God-image; rather, each of us reflects the creator in a unique way.

God is a God of turning things around, this thing we call 're-demption', which means we can go to the manufacturer for repair! When we step into a life with him, we become a new creation. This does not mean all of our life experiences are voided and our culture is lost. What it does mean is that our guilt and shame have been slaughtered at the cross and our suffering is met with his love. We are now free to walk step by step towards becoming the person he intended us to be.

Psalm 139.1–18

I am known

You have searched me, LORD,
and you know me.
You know when I sit and when I rise;
you perceive my thoughts from afar.
You discern my going out and my lying down;
you are familiar with all my ways.
Before a word is on my tongue
you, LORD, know it completely.
You hem me in behind and before,
and you lay your hand upon me.
Such knowledge is too wonderful for me,
too lofty for me to attain.

Where can I go from your Spirit?
Where can I flee from your presence?
If I go up to the heavens, you are there;
if I make my bed in the depths, you are there.
If I rise on the wings of the dawn,
if I settle on the far side of the sea,
even there your hand will guide me,
your right hand will hold me fast.
If I say, 'Surely the darkness will hide me
and the light become night around me,'
even the darkness will not be dark to you;

the night will shine like the day,
for darkness is as light to you.

For you created my inmost being;
you knit me together in my mother's womb.
I praise you because I am fearfully and wonderfully made;
your works are wonderful,
I know that full well.
My frame was not hidden from you
when I was made in the secret place,
when I was woven together in the depths of the earth.
Your eyes saw my unformed body;
all the days ordained for me were written in your book
before one of them came to be.
How precious to me are your thoughts, God!
How vast is the sum of them!
Were I to count them,
they would outnumber the grains of sand –
when I awake, I am still with you.

Day 8

His perfection held within our imperfection

In the Bible, one of the early believers in Jesus, Paul, talks about the fact that we carry our 'treasure in jars of clay'. It is in the brokenness and disorder of our lives that God shines through. As our maker masterfully puts us back together, his treasure is poured into our lives. He has not come so we might live a half-life but that we might live life to the full, our jar spilling over with his love and life. No matter what we have gone through, or are indeed still going through (because God never promised us an easy life!), he is going to make sure that he shines through us in and through it all.

It has been said that we have a God-shaped void within us, and when we encounter him and realize that he is real, this void is filled. The part of the jigsaw we could never locate is finally in place. We have found our creator and he is here to bind up our broken places. As we begin to discover his character and nature and ponder him in all his perfection, things start to change in us. We begin to be transformed – not by our own effort but by simply focusing on him and his life-giving power and compassion. Bit by bit, he takes our brokenness and begins to heal us. He helps us to make sense of some of the experiences we have gone through, and where there simply are no answers, he helps us to find a place of peace.

He leads us towards a more transparent life, not a perfect life. Allowing others to see the cracks in the clay can make us feel vulnerable, but God doesn't need us to be fake; rather, he helps us with our weak areas. In fact, the Bible says of God, 'My strength comes into its own in your weakness' (2 Cor. 12.9, MSG). For some, it is a relief to not have to keep up the charade any longer. We can identify with his lost, broken and hurting world.

Kintsugi is the Japanese art of repairing broken pottery with lacquer dusted or mixed with powdered gold. Its breakage and repair are seen as part of the history of its life, rather than something to disguise. When the vase is restored, it is more beautiful for the story that it tells; the gold in the cracks makes it even more precious. So it is with us.

Remember, it is not our strength and outward appearance that make us 'good Christians'. God does not need a PR machine. The simple act of trusting him allows him to be seen by us, in us and through us.

2 Corinthians 4.7–12 (MSG)

Treasure in jars of clay

If you only look at *us*, you might well miss the brightness. We carry this precious Message around in the unadorned clay pots of our ordinary lives. That's to prevent anyone from confusing God's incomparable power with us.

Day 9

Trauma and emotional healing

What was the worst moment of your life?

You may have had more than one.

Sometimes these moments can stretch into hours, days, weeks and years. They push us off balance, rip down our boundaries and leave us numb, bruised and dislocated from ourselves.

This is called trauma.

It could be caused by sexual, physical, mental or emotional abuse.

It could be caused by loneliness, neglect or the threat of physical violence.

We will often do *anything* to avoid feeling that way again.

We tend to avoid situations or people that remind us of our trauma because those old feelings can come rushing back in a tsunami of pain.

The story we are looking at today, of the son who leaves home, shows all the signs of trauma.

We don't know why he demands his inheritance and runs away from home. But once he has spent all the money, he is left to face his own emptiness, isolation and pain. He is treated like dirt and hits rock bottom. He is separated from everything that was his identity.

The only thing that can heal this kind of pain is love.

God's love is bigger and stronger than the trauma. When the son returns home, expecting punishment, his father runs to embrace him, to hold him. The trauma and pain of loneliness is exchanged for love and acceptance.

This is a picture of how God responds to our trauma. There is no blame, punishment, 'I told you so' or rejection. Just complete love and acceptance. That's it. And this is where the healing begins.

Think of it like a formula:

Trauma = isolation and separation
Healing = love, welcome and inclusion

God's love and acceptance, expressed through his family (what some call church) can also act as medicine to heal trauma.

Love turns the lonely outsiders into guests of honour at their own welcome parties!

Where to get help

HPS (Healing Prayer School): https://www.healingprayerschool.org.uk/contact

Samaritans: www.samaritans.org

Luke 15.11–32 (MSG)

The prodigal son

Then he said, 'There was once a man who had two sons. The younger said to his father, "Father, I want right now what's coming to me."

'So the father divided the property between them. It wasn't long before the younger son packed his bags and left for a distant country. There, undisciplined and dissipated, he wasted everything he had. After he had gone through all his money, there was a bad famine all through that country and he began to feel it. He signed on with a citizen there who assigned him to his fields to slop the pigs. He was so hungry he would have eaten the corn-cobs in the pig slop, but no one would give him any.

'That brought him to his senses. He said, "All those farmhands working for my father sit down to three meals a day, and here I am starving to death. I'm going back to my father.

I'll say to him, Father, I've sinned against God, I've sinned before you; I don't deserve to be called your son. Take me on as a hired hand." He got right up and went home to his father.

'When he was still a long way off, his father saw him. His heart pounding, he ran out, embraced him, and kissed him. The son started his speech: "Father, I've sinned against God, I've sinned before you; I don't deserve to be called your son ever again."

'But the father wasn't listening. He was calling to the servants, "Quick. Bring a clean set of clothes and dress him. Put the family ring on his finger and sandals on his feet. Then get a prize-winning heifer and roast it. We're going to feast! We're going to have a wonderful time! My son is here – given up for dead and now alive! Given up for lost and now found!" And they began to have a wonderful time.

'All this time his older son was out in the field. When the day's work was done he came in. As he approached the house, he heard the music and dancing. Calling over one of the houseboys, he asked what was going on. He told him, "Your brother came home. Your father has ordered a feast – barbecued beef! – because he has him home safe and sound."

'The older brother stomped off in an angry sulk and refused to join in. His father came out and tried to talk to him, but he wouldn't listen. The son said, "Look how many years I've stayed here serving you, never giving you one moment of grief, but have you ever thrown a party for me and my friends? Then this son of yours who has thrown away your money on whores shows up and you go all out with a feast!"

'His father said, "Son, you don't understand. You're with me all the time, and everything that is mine is yours – but this is a wonderful time, and we had to celebrate. This brother of yours was dead, and he's alive! He was lost, and he's found!"'

Day 10

Overcoming fear

What are you afraid of? What is unresolved? Do you currently have anything that is scaring you?

It's easy to sing, 'Don't worry, be happy,' but fear often robs us of anything that resembles happiness. A sense of dread sits in the pit of our stomach, tightens our chest and leaves us feeling weighed down. We're unable to see things clearly and can be overwhelmed by fear. In these moments, it's hard not to let panic or immobilization overtake us.

Fear distorts the truth and has us focus on what might happen instead of what is actually happening in the here and now. So what truths will help us counteract fear when it's placed our bodies in lockdown?

Facing fear is not the denial of reality and labelling it 'faith'; it is finding whatever resources we can to turn our natural 'freeze' reaction into 'fight' or 'flight'. When we are walking with God, discovering or returning to the truths we know about God's nature and character are fundamental in this process. Knowing that whatever happens in our lives, these truths remain: God is in control, God loves me, God is good, God has a plan for my life.

The Bible tells us that perfect love casts out fear. How does that work? God wants a relationship of love with us, and when we experience his love at the deepest level, our trust grows, our hope begins to spring up and the resilience to face even the most difficult of circumstances starts to develop. This is no easy walk or quick fix, but it is possible.

Romans 8.31 says, 'What, then, shall we say in response to these things? If God is for us, who can be against us?'

The all-powerful, infinite God is in our corner. He has our back. He steps up and steps into our situations. He protects us. He gives us courage.

So if we know God has got our back, what is there to be scared of?

The hold that fear has had on our lives can be broken. We can be set free when we ask Jesus, but we may still need to exercise this new-found freedom in our daily walk. Here are some additional approaches that may help this process:

- Try journalling about the times when God has already answered prayers and dissolved fear. He helped before; he can help again.
- Reach out to trusted friends for emotional support, to pray with or to talk the fear through.
- Work on your mindset. In counselling, one approach is around creating new positive neural pathways in our brains. Often, 'fear motorways' lead to destinations that don't serve us well. Instead of allowing our mind to travel down its normal path of fear, we may, over time develop new roads, leading to healthier mindset destinations. The Bible says, 'Be transformed by the renewing of your mind' (Rom. 12.2).

Fear, pack your bags. God is for us. The all-powerful, infinite God is in our corner.

Philippians 4.6–7 (MSG)

Don't fret or worry. Instead of worrying, pray. Let petitions and praises shape your worries into prayers, letting God know your concerns. Before you know it, a sense of God's wholeness, everything coming together for good, will come and settle you down. It's wonderful what happens when Christ displaces worry at the center of your life.

1 John 4.16–19

God is love. Whoever lives in love lives in God, and God in them. This is how love is made complete among us so that we will have confidence on the day of judgement: in this world we are like Jesus. There is no fear in love. But perfect love drives out fear, because fear has to do with punishment. The one who fears is not made perfect in love.

We love because he first loved us.

Day 11

The relationship of the Trinity

Fundamental to the Christian faith is the concept of the Trinity – that is, the three-in-one God. God as Parent, God as Son and Saviour, and God as Holy Spirit, the constant presence.

From the beginning, in creation, we see the three working together. 'In the beginning God created the heavens and the earth. Now the earth was formless and empty, darkness was over the surface of the deep, and the Spirit of God was hovering over the waters' (Gen. 1.1).

Then, John 1.1–3, where John describes Jesus as the Word, says, 'In the beginning was the Word, and the Word was with God, and the Word was God. He was with God in the beginning. Through him all things were made; without him nothing was made that has been made.'

In our twenty-first-century societal structure, it's very easy to over-separate things. People may think of God the Father as the boss, the one who is really running the show and the main player. Jesus runs the PR department; he's the face of the campaign. The Holy Spirit does all that touchy-feely stuff, hovering somewhere in the background.

In reality, all three are equal players and are of equal status, but all have distinctive characteristics.

In the Bible, in various ways, Jesus talks about doing what the Father tells him to do, suggesting subordination to a higher authority. This can lead us into thinking that Jesus is somehow inferior, but we must understand this is Divine God in human form taking on human likeness and frailty in order to win back humanity. God steps into the disordered mess and offers relationship. God leaves his unlimited form and becomes limited for a while here on earth in the human shape of Jesus. In that limited form, God is subject to human limitations such as cold, heat, hunger, thirst and pain.

Jesus says he and the Father are one and the same – 'Anyone who has seen me has seen the Father' (John 14.9) – and yet, in the form of Jesus, God laid down his status, aligned himself to us with empathy and compassion, and climbed under the skin of humanity even to the point of being tortured by crucifixion. If Jesus had simply died, we would say, 'Wow what a guy; he really loved us; he was the best of us.' But, being God, Jesus never lost sight of his divinity – he could not be less than who he truly is. He could not deny his power. He beat death, rising from the dead and making a way for humanity to be in eternal relationship with the three-in-one God. He overcame the human condition and makes us co-winners alongside him.

On leaving the earth in flesh-form, God does not leave us alone, rejected and bereft. He still wants the personalization of who he is to be felt and so he sends the Holy Spirit to comfort, direct and speak to us in many and various ways. The Bible says the Spirit is poured out on *all* people (Joel 2.28). When we move towards Jesus, we become alive to the Holy Spirit, who shows us the truth, opens our eyes and directs us towards completeness.

At the centre of the three-in-one God relationship is surrender. The Godhead's surrender to itself is profound, and it is the perfect example of love, trust and unity.

Colossians 1.15–17

The Son is the image of the invisible God, the firstborn over all creation. For in him all things were created: things in heaven and on earth, visible and invisible, whether thrones or powers or rulers or authorities; all things have been created through him and for him. He is before all things, and in him all things hold together.

John 14.16–17

And I will ask the Father, and he will give you another advocate to help you and be with you forever – the Spirit of truth. The world cannot accept him, because it neither sees him nor knows him. But you know him, for he lives with you and will be in you.

Day 12
Jesus' death

There is nothing nice to say about death, and there is certainly nothing nice to say about a barbaric, torturous and prolonged death on a wooden structure. People generally don't like to ponder the subject, and as a society we tend to sanitize death, keeping it as a private and intimate affair. But it was Jesus Christ's public execution that secured our relationship with God. It was the cost of forgiveness for all the depravity, immorality and wickedness of the world, so that all the selfish, wayward, cruel and damaging acts that are perpetuated by people could be eliminated and forgiven, allowing us, the unholy, to be made holy and to have a relationship with our Father in heaven. This is God Almighty, who is love personified. He had to endure the humiliating death of his most Beloved Son, so that he could be unified with us forever.

Unexpected? Not at all! We learn throughout the Old Testament, thousands of years before Jesus was even born, that God had been hatching a plan to reunite humanity with himself.

The blueprint was first made in Genesis 22, when God instructed Abraham to sacrifice Isaac on an altar and then swapped his son for a sheep. The significance of this only becomes clear when we understand that it was part of a carefully constructed divine pattern, one that points to the redeeming sacrifice of Jesus (called the Lamb of God) upon the cross many years later.

In the Jewish Scriptures, the book of Leviticus tells us that it was only when people had been cleansed by a sacrificial lamb that they could draw near to God to worship him and to celebrate his presence. This ritual foretells the coming of Jesus Christ, who offers himself as a perfect, once-for-all sacrifice so that each one of us might have a relationship with God forever.

But perhaps the passage that gives one of the clearest explanations behind the death of Jesus is Isaiah 53. Here we see how God, who exists outside time, reaches down into humankind's timeline to pull together the threads of a tapestry that explain the coming of Jesus and the significance of his death on the cross even before the events occurred. The reason: the event and its consequences provide us with a bright future and the possibility of eternal life. Woven together in the poetic words of Isaiah, we are told the story of how a righteous servant, despised yet loving perfectly, would suffer a cruel and brutal execution even though he had done nothing wrong. He would be accountable for all the wrongdoing of the world so that we could stand sinless before our God.

Eight hundred years later, Jesus died, and his blood was spilled so that those who were before him, and those coming after him, could be righteous and united in peace with God.

Isaiah 53.2–7, 9 (MSG)

The Messiah's death foretold

There was nothing attractive about him,
nothing to cause us to take a second look.
He was looked down on and passed over,
a man who suffered, who knew pain firsthand.
One look at him and people turned away.
We looked down on him, thought he was scum.
But the fact is, it was *our* pains he carried –
our disfigurements, all the things wrong with *us*.
We thought he brought it on himself,
that God was punishing him for his own failures.
But it was *our* sins that did that to him,
that ripped and tore and crushed him – *our* sins!

Jesus' death

He took the punishment, and that made us whole.
Through his bruises we get healed.
We're all like sheep who've wandered off and gotten lost.
We've all done our own thing, gone our own way.
And GOD has piled all our sins, everything we've done
      wrong,
on him, on him.

He was beaten, he was tortured,
but he didn't say a word . . .
They buried him with the wicked,
threw him in a grave with a rich man,
Even though he'd never hurt a soul
or said one word that wasn't true.

Day 13

The resurrection

Jesus had been executed by the Romans and was buried in a tomb with a huge boulder rolled across it. As if that wasn't enough, two guards were posted to watch the tomb. This was all to make sure Jesus' followers didn't sneak into the tomb and steal the body. Then they could have proclaimed that Jesus had come back to life and must be who he said he was: the Son of God.

There are some things about this story that mean Jesus did come back to life and conquer death. If the Christians had made up the story, why would they have been so surprised when they heard Jesus wasn't in the tomb? If they were making up the story, they would not have come up with the idea that a woman (in those days considered an unreliable witness) would be the one to find the empty tomb. But most of all, when Christians started getting killed in large numbers by the Romans for their faith, why did they not just say it was all a hoax? Would you die for something you knew wasn't true?

And there is another point about this story. Mary Magdalene didn't recognize the risen Jesus. She had gone on tour with him, eaten with him and was his friend, but at that moment she thought he was the gardener.

Maybe we meet Jesus in lots of ways and places and don't recognize him – in the friendship of others, in the beauty of nature and creativity. Are there times when you think you may have met Jesus and not recognized him?

The resurrection happened.

Jesus took the worst pain and suffering the world could dish out, and it killed him.

And then . . .

He came back to life.

Christians celebrate this at Easter.

Why? Because it means that Jesus is more powerful than suffering and death. However bad it gets for us, he has been there and been through it. And his life in us will also take us through darkness and into light.

At first, after the resurrection, he appeared to his friends like a regular person. But then he went back to heaven, and in a mysterious way he continues to hold 'all things . . . together' (Col. 1.17). He holds us together. He is fully alive, fully with us. Jesus is at the centre of it all.

John 20.1–17

The empty tomb

Early on the first day of the week, while it was still dark, Mary Magdalene went to the tomb and saw that the stone had been removed from the entrance. So she came running to Simon Peter and the other disciple, the one Jesus loved, and said, 'They have taken the Lord out of the tomb, and we don't know where they have put him!'

So Peter and the other disciple started for the tomb. Both were running, but the other disciple outran Peter and reached the tomb first. He bent over and looked in at the strips of linen lying there but did not go in. Then Simon Peter came along behind him and went straight into the tomb. He saw the strips of linen lying there, as well as the cloth that had been wrapped around Jesus' head. The cloth was still lying in its place, separate from the linen. Finally the other disciple, who had reached the tomb first, also went inside. He saw and believed. (They still did not understand from Scripture that Jesus had to rise from the dead.) Then the disciples went back to where they were staying.

Jesus appears to Mary Magdalene

Now Mary stood outside the tomb crying. As she wept, she bent over to look into the tomb and saw two angels in white, seated where Jesus' body had been, one at the head and the other at the foot.

They asked her, 'Woman, why are you crying?'

'They have taken my Lord away,' she said, 'and I don't know where they have put him.' At this, she turned around and saw Jesus standing there, but she did not realize that it was Jesus.

He asked her, 'Woman, why are you crying? Who is it you are looking for?'

Thinking he was the gardener, she said, 'Sir, if you have carried him away, tell me where you have put him, and I will get him.'

Jesus said to her, 'Mary.'

She turned towards him and cried out in Aramaic, 'Rabboni!' (which means 'Teacher').

Day 14
The Holy Spirit

When Jesus was baptized, 'the Holy Spirit descended from heaven in the form of a dove and landed on him'.

In the above passage we have Jesus who is being baptized, the Father who says, 'This is my son . . . with him I am well pleased' (Matt. 3.17) and the Holy Spirit who lands on Jesus in the form of a dove. Christians describe these three as Trinity.

But what, or who, is the Holy Spirit in this Trinity?

The Holy Spirit is the tangible, life-changing and life-giving presence and power of God. But this is not just an energy source, like a mobile phone power pack. This is a person.

The Spirit is represented by different symbols in the Bible – sometimes as a peace-bringing dove, sometimes as wind, sometimes as fire. All these symbols highlight the free, wild and transformative nature of the Spirit. We often perceive the presence of the Spirit by the effect on things we can see, in a similar way as we perceive the wind as it blows through leaves on the trees.

It was the Spirit landing on Jesus' disciples like a fireball that ignited the worldwide movement we now call church (Acts 2.1–4). This fire turned scared, timid people into world-changing warriors. This supernatural energy does not come from within us. We receive the Spirit when we surrender to Christ and accept that we are no longer running the show. It is the Spirit who empowers us to produce the fruit of love, peace and joy, regardless of how badly our lives may be going. The Spirit gives gifts to the whole church to help us grow as the people of God. This includes the ability to speak in a prayer language different from our normal speech, as well as sometimes being able to heal and do miracles.

Relying on the Holy Spirit is like jumping into a river and letting the current direct us. We can listen to what Spirit is saying to us in dreams, in our thoughts, through the Bible and through other people. We need to keep our spiritual ears open for the wisdom that comes directly from the Spirit. The more we listen, the more we recognize the Spirit's voice.

The Spirit is also all about bringing peace and reconciliation. This is the symbol of the dove again. People often think in terms of us and them, in or out, right or wrong. Sadly, the church can also make some people the insiders and others the outsiders. The Holy Spirit never operates in this binary way. The Spirit is to be found moving *between* people and *through* people. The Spirit cannot be pinned down by anyone's version of right or wrong. The Spirit is a dancer, always moving between and through us, creating communities rooted in God's love, reconciliation and peace.

To be church means joining in with the dancing Spirit who is always linking our hands and hearts together to show humanity what God *really* looks like.

Luke 3.21–22 (TPT)

Jesus' baptism

One day, Jesus came to be baptized along with all the others. As he was consumed with the spirit of prayer, the heavenly realm ripped open above him and the Holy Spirit descended from heaven in the form of a dove and landed on him. Then God's audible voice was heard, saying, 'My Son, you are my beloved one. Through you I am fulfilled.'

Day 15
Faith in action (part 1)

With God living in us, our lives begin to be transformed. This is a natural outcome of getting to know God. The more we experience the transformation, the more we trust, and the more we trust, the hungrier we get to see more of him in and through our lives – the change is exciting. There comes a point when all this transformation in us begins to spill out into the world around us and we become conduits of change just by being our new and transformed selves. Our will is lining up with God's will.

This can be exercised in any number of ways:

Loving our neighbour

We can see in Matthew 22.37–39 that there is a fluid cycle at work. We love God, and as we begin to grow in our knowledge of his love for us, we begin more and more to love ourselves. We begin to see our neighbours as God sees them and then we begin to love them too. This is not about rules or good behaviour. A by-product of learning to love ourselves is that we begin to treat both ourselves and those around us in a more respectful way and with a more generous spirit. When asked, 'Who is my neighbour?', Jesus replied with a story about a man who was mugged and beaten (Luke 10.25–37). The people from his own culture crossed the road and ignored him, yet a stranger from a hostile culture helped him. Then Jesus asked, 'Who was this man's neighbour?' When he asks us the same question, the answer is, everybody to whom we can show compassion, empathy and kindness. Our love, kindness and generosity are meant for all.

Prayer

Prayer works. Prayer changes things. The Bible says in Ephesians 6.12, 'For our struggle is not against flesh and blood, but against the rulers, against the authorities, against the powers of this dark world and against the spiritual forces of evil in the heavenly realms.' Our prayers should not be against people but against the brokenness and darkness that cause hurtful actions.

When Jesus died and rose again, the Bible says he overcame death and darkness once and for all (Heb. 9.26–28). It also says that we can break the power behind this pain and wickedness (Eph. 6.12), and we do this when we pray in the name of Jesus. When the Bible says 'in the name of Jesus', it's not saying we have to quote the name to release some kind of magic. It's using an ancient phrase that means 'with the authority of', as used when saying, 'Stop in the name of the King.' It denotes that the believers have the authority to bring darkness down. The unified prayer of believers, understanding God's will, can bring about phenomenal change in the world on both a micro and a macro scale.

James 2.14–18 (MSG)

Dear friends, do you think you'll get anywhere in this if you learn all the right words but never do anything? Does merely talking about faith indicate that a person really has it? For instance, you come upon an old friend dressed in rags and half-starved and say, 'Good morning, friend! Be clothed in Christ! Be filled with the Holy Spirit!' and walk off without providing so much as a coat or a cup of soup – where does that get you? Isn't it obvious that God-talk without God-acts is outrageous nonsense?

I can already hear one of you agreeing by saying, 'Sounds good. You take care of the faith department, I'll handle the works department.'

Not so fast. You can no more show me your works apart from your faith than I can show you my faith apart from my works. Faith and works, works and faith, fit together hand in glove.

Day 16
Faith in action (part 2)

As we continue to look at faith in action, we turn to what it truly means to share one's faith.

Some may think of this as a missionary going to a far-off land to tell people about Jesus; others may think of it as standing on a street corner and preaching the gospel. Some might even consider that it is the job of the preacher in the church. Sharing our faith doesn't have to be preaching, although there are those who have this gift.

So, what is it?

It's going and telling the good news and it's *being* good news. It's a kind of 'Show and Tell', as it involves not just telling others about God's love but showing love too. Telling and being 'good news' presupposes that we have some good news to share! It's sharing what we've experienced and the truth we have discovered. Faith in action is pouring out to others the love that God has poured into us. It's also allowing others to enter the debate if they have a different view, remembering we weren't always so certain. It involves listening. A lot.

One of the first people to see Jesus after he had risen was Mary Magdalene. The Bible tells us that she went to tell the disciples the good news (John 20.18), making her the first evangelist of the risen Jesus. (The original meaning of the word evangelist was 'bringer of good news'.) She had an encounter and couldn't keep it to herself; it needed to be shared, and out of the overflow of this experience she quite literally ran to tell others.

When our lives are changed by Jesus, we begin to love others and desire for them to experience the same freedom we have experienced. We cannot drag someone who doesn't believe in Jesus kicking and screaming to our view – believers who want to share their faith wait patiently, become lovingly present with those around them, and wait for the questions. Sharing is not about manipulating conversation and shoehorning our beliefs. It is about living alongside one another, loving people and, when asked, being able to give a reason for the hope that lives in us. It is a work of God through the Holy Spirit.

There's not a special way of doing this, and it's not a matter of being erudite and clever. The Bible says that out of the overflow of the heart the mouth speaks.

Luke 6.45

A good man brings good things out of the good stored up in his heart, and an evil man brings evil things out of the evil stored up in his heart. For the mouth speaks what the heart is full of.

1 Peter 3.15

But in your hearts revere Christ as Lord. Always be prepared to give an answer to everyone who asks you to give the reason for the hope that you have. But do this with gentleness and respect.

Day 17
Praise and worship

Praise and worship are a huge part of our identity as followers of Jesus, both individually and corporately, whether it's through song, music, dance or any other form of creativity. But that's just a slice of the pie. Worship is words and actions. Worship is anything in our lives that honours God. Worship is connection to God, from our recognition of his ultimate power and greatness (praise) to our adoration of him – giving thanks for all he has done and giving ourselves to him over and over (worship).

The Oxford English Dictionary describes worship as, 'Show reverence and adoration for (a deity); feel great admiration or devotion for.'[2]

We are communicating:

- This is who you are (no matter what I face in my life);
- Thank you for all you have done (no matter how large or small);
- I surrender to you (I entrust my hopes and dreams, all I am and all I have, to you).

As we worship, we take stock, we tune in, we put things straight and find our true north. It's a great way of getting our eyes fixed on Jesus – raising our sights.

I lift up my eyes to the mountains –
where does my help come from?
My help comes from the LORD,
the Maker of heaven and earth.
(Ps. 121.1–2)

Through our praise and worship, we look to him in surrender (worship), or we recognize and acknowledge who he is (praise). In these actions we begin to see the story of God at work in our lives and how he has been holding us throughout.

Ephesians 1.11 reminds us, 'It's in Christ that we find out who we are and what we are living for' (MSG).

Praise and worship can be quiet and reflective, it can be 'barn-storming', and it can be all stages in between. We can praise and worship God with our face shining with happiness or through tears of grief. However it happens, it's important to remember the WOW!

> Everyone was amazed and gave praise to God. They were filled with awe and said, 'We have seen remarkable things today.'
> (Luke 5.26)

N. T. Wright hit the nail on the head when he said, 'When you begin to glimpse the reality of God, the natural reaction is to worship him.'[3]

Psalm 136.1–9 (MSG)

A psalm of thanksgiving
Thank GOD! He deserves your thanks.
His love never quits.
Thank the God of all gods,
His love never quits.
Thank the Lord of all lords.
His love never quits.
Thank the miracle-working God,
His love never quits.
The God whose skill formed the cosmos,
His love never quits.
The God who laid out earth on ocean foundations,
His love never quits.

The God who filled the skies with light,
His love never quits.
The sun to watch over the day,
His love never quits.
Moon and stars as guardians of the night,
His love never quits.

Day 18

The power of forgiveness

Forgiveness works in three areas: being forgiven, forgiving ourselves and forgiving others. Today, we'll just look at the first two.

When we first encounter God, he invites us to recognize our imperfection, to acknowledge that there are things we have done wrong or that we do wrong or omit to do right. For some, the overwhelming sense of shame never allows us to be able to admit this wrong. To admit we are wrong tips us into crash mode. If I am wrong, then I am a terrible person. No, if you've done something wrong you are just being human.

The Bible says that everyone has sinned and all fall short of God's ideal (Rom. 3.23).

But the Bible also tells us, 'There is now no condemnation for those who are in Christ Jesus' (Rom. 8.1). This means that God is making a distinction between admitting wrongdoing and shame. It is only because of his love that we can bring our imperfection to him. We can come boldly and with confidence to our loving Father. He will not throw it back in our face; he will not use it against us or hold on to it. There is no shame in Jesus.

Shame is the appendix of the soul, the totally unnecessary, good-for-nothing trait, but when we give it voice, it has the power to control our lives.

There was a story of an elderly lady who went to her pastor saying, 'I've done something so bad and God cannot forgive me for this. I have carried this thing for years.'

The pastor assured her that God would have forgiven her.

She answered, 'If God has forgiven me, then you pray about it and ask God what it was I did all those years ago and ask him if he forgives me.'

The pastor went away, and the next week the elderly lady appeared again and asked, 'What did God say? What was it I did? Did you hear from God? Does he forgive me?'

'Yes,' the pastor replied, 'I asked God what it was you had done.'

The woman bowed her head in shame.

The pastor continued, 'And God said he can't remember.'

This is what our God is like. Psalm 103.12 says, 'As far as the east is from the west, so far has He removed our wrongdoings from us' (NASB).

Sometimes it's more about us letting go and forgiving ourselves.

The Bible tells us that those who have been forgiven much, love much (Luke 7.47, paraphrased). When we let go of our need to look perfect and admit our vulnerability and wrongdoing, we make space for more of God's love to be poured in. He doesn't ask us to bring our wrongdoing to him so that we can be transformed into being in a constant state of shame and self-loathing. He asks us to come as we are, warts and all, and he will love us and he will pour his forgiveness and acceptance into us. It's done.

No guilt – no shame

There is no condemnation for those who are in Christ Jesus.

Romans 8.1–4 (MSG)

With the arrival of Jesus, the Messiah, that fateful dilemma is resolved. Those who enter into Christ's being-here-for-us no longer have to live under a continuous, low-lying black cloud. A new power is in operation. The Spirit of life in Christ, like a strong wind, has magnificently cleared the air, freeing you from a fated lifetime of brutal tyranny at the hands of sin and death.

God went for the jugular when he sent his own Son. He didn't deal with the problem as something remote and unimportant. In his Son, Jesus, he personally took on the human condition, entered the disordered mess of struggling humanity in order to set it right once and for all. The law code, weakened as it always was by fractured human nature, could never have done that.

The law always ended up being used as a Band-Aid on sin instead of a deep healing of it. And now what the law code asked for but we couldn't deliver is accomplished as we, instead of redoubling our own efforts, simply embrace what the Spirit is doing in us.

Day 19
Forgiving others

It is in God's nature to redeem. This part of God's nature infuses everything he does; it is constant. Redeeming relationships or helping us to recover our emotional world is all part of the redemptive experience.

Forgiving others is both a choice and a journey, a decision and a way of life. We do not need to deny the hurt or the wrong behaviour towards us. We do not need to break it down into bite-sized, manageable chunks or minimize it in order that we can cope. We can be empowered to forgive wholesale. Forgiving others sets *us* free from the burden of having to think about the situation over and over – it frees *us* from the relentless nature of being constantly triggered by past wounds.

Letting go

In some instances, it is wise to let the person go. We can do no more. They may have passed on, have moved on or be reluctant to make peace with us. That's not our responsibility. Our only responsibility is to forgive those who hurt us and then let go.

In other instances, God brings us to a place where restoration is possible. These times are truly miraculous. Relationships we would never have thought could change sometimes do. Obviously, this is not wise in all situations, and we should seek counsel and not be afraid to make decisions either way.

Taking offence

If we are black-and-white thinkers, we can easily demonize those who have hurt us. We are the goodies and they are the baddies.

The truth is, sometimes they overlap; sometimes situations are more complex than good or bad, right or wrong. Fallings-out can sometimes be nuanced but the pain is always real.

Most day-to-day unforgiveness has its roots in offence. Offence was given or taken and for some reason we can't get past how that makes us feel. The next stage is to declare the offender 100 per cent wrong, they are totally wicked and have no redeeming qualities. And the following stage is to drag others in to take sides in the fray.

Abuse

Having said this – sometimes the wrongdoing to us (or to someone we love) is completely one-sided (such as physical, sexual or emotional abuse). In these cases we are not guilty, but we do need to set ourselves free from the abuser. We cannot carry the weight of the tormentor on our shoulders, but God can. In this instance, it is more about handing the abuser over into the hands of God, letting go and allowing God to deal with that person.

Step one is making the choice to forgive. In some ways, this may be the easiest part. The second step is to walk that process out until the residues of trauma, hurt and bitterness have shifted and we can come to a place of poignancy. Do not be afraid to ask for help and prayer. It can take time.

One thing is for sure: God does not want us to remain bitter, broken and living a half-life. He wants us to be free.

Colossians 3.12–15 (MSG)

Forgiving others

So, chosen by God for this new life of love, dress in the wardrobe God picked out for you: compassion, kindness, humility, quiet strength, discipline. Be even-tempered, content with second place, quick to forgive an offense. Forgive as quickly and completely as the Master forgave you. And regardless of what else you put on, wear love. It's your basic, all-purpose garment. Never be without it.

Let the peace of Christ keep you in tune with each other, in step with each other. None of this going off and doing your own thing. And cultivate thankfulness.

Day 20
Where is my past?

When we start to relate to Christ not just as a historical figure or a religious idea but as *our* personal reality, we have become a new creation. It says in the Bible that the old has gone and the new has come (2 Cor. 5.17). This raises the question, though, what has happened to our past? Does our history, family, upbringing, culture and past trauma just disappear? Gone up in a puff of smoke?

For many years, I thought the answer to this question was yes. I was taught in church that all my old ways of thinking, all my bad habits, my fears and my worries were now a thing of the past. All I needed was Christ. Like a pantomime joke, 'Where's my past?' 'Behind you!' The only problem was that I *was* still massively influenced by my upbringing and past trauma. No amount of praying, reading the Bible and trying harder made any difference to my anxieties and low self-esteem. So my past was still very much with me.

But it says in the verse today that I died and now my life is hidden in Christ. How do we make sense of this?

I now believe that this verse is not asking us to deny our past or pretend it never happened. This kind of denial can lead to a lot of psychological problems. If bad stuff has happened, that has to be acknowledged. The effects may still be playing out. For instance, the self I developed in reaction to my history, the defences and self-sufficient ways of coping and defending myself from further hurt, this self (what some call the false self) needed to be surrendered. We are not equipped to run our lives on our own, and walking with Jesus means surrendering ourselves to Christ. This doesn't eradicate our identity, as some seem to teach. It means that Christ now shines through the cracks in our history and redeems all the pain and trauma in our unique and Christ-shaped selves.

Being in Christ enables us to relate to our past with compassion, to grieve what needs to be grieved, to forgive what needs to be forgiven, to make peace with our own history. We are no longer defined by our past because now we have become the expression of Christ in our own unique and unrepeatable form.

Colossians 3.3

Death to self

For you died, and your life is now hidden with Christ in God.

Day 21
Heaven and eternity

The Oxford English Dictionary defines the word 'eternal' as 'Lasting or existing forever; without end'.[4] So, what is eternal life? Jesus described it this way:

> Now this is eternal life: that they know you, the only true God, and Jesus Christ, whom you have sent.
> (John 17.3)

These words of Jesus speak of an intimate relationship with God that grows and deepens and is a relationship that, once begun, never ends. So where does heaven come into all of this?

Most of us think of heaven and earth as two entirely separate realms. Earth is where we live now, and heaven is where we will go when we die. But that's not what the early church believed. The first followers of Jesus saw 'heaven' and 'earth' as God's space and ours – if you like, as the twin halves of God's creation. They believed that God would finally bring heaven and earth together in a great act of new creation, by bringing an end to death, mourning, pain, sickness and suffering. They believed that God would then raise his people from the dead, to share in this rescued and renewed creation.

They believed that, with the resurrection of Jesus, this new creation had already been launched. Jesus embodied in himself the perfect fusion of heaven and earth. The point was not just for us to 'go to heaven', but for the life of heaven to arrive on earth.

We know from the words of Jesus that heaven is the place of eternal life with God. It is a place of rest and peace, and it lasts forever.

We also know that, while Jesus is preparing heaven for us in the life to come, he is also preparing us for heaven in this life.

The concept of heaven and earth being so close is reflected in the temple in Jerusalem. Only the priests were permitted to go into the holy of holies section where, once a year, they would make a sacrifice for the sin of the nation. This most holy place was behind a thick curtain. When Jesus died on the cross, the temple curtain was torn in two, signifying that the ultimate sacrifice had been made and as a result the divide between God and us no longer exists.

The implications of heaven here on earth are profound, perhaps suggesting that we don't always access as much of God as we could, and that an even closer relationship is available.

John 14.1–4

Do not let your hearts be troubled. You believe in God; believe also in me. My Father's house has many rooms; if that were not so, would I have told you that I am going there to prepare a place for you? And if I go and prepare a place for you, I will come back and take you to be with me that you also may be where I am. You know the way to the place where I am going.

Day 22
Faith that lasts

Jesus often spoke in parables, drawing the interest of his listeners with stories relating to their everyday lives. Often he would tell a story without explaining its full meaning there and then. He would leave the crowds longing for more, encouraging them to discuss, dissect and work out its meaning.

In the parable about the sower, Jesus talked about a farmer who goes out to plant seeds. The seeds fall on four different types of land:

- On the path;
- On rocky places;
- Among thorns;
- In fertile soil.

Jesus likened this to how we may experience faith in him and his kingdom.

The seed that falls on the path cannot establish roots so is quickly stolen; the truth is missed, robbed in the blink of an eye.

The seed that falls on the rocky soil is unable to grow deep roots, and the moment trouble comes it cannot withstand the struggle; it does not have the strength it takes to continue to believe.

The seed that falls among thorns speaks of those who worry about life and money. They are most concerned with and distracted by material things.

The seed that falls on fertile soil digs its roots down, grows upward and produces a harvest that far outweighs the initial investment.

Even those seeds that have been planted in nutrient-rich ground can waver, have bad seasons and struggle, but if the roots have gone down far enough they will ultimately remain planted. The way to avoid the first three outcomes is to:

- Remain curious – if we are hungry to find the truth, we will indeed find it;
- Persevere – through the trials and tests of life;
- Stay focused – don't get distracted by the things the world throws at us: money, status and all the things we can 'get'.

Be safe in the knowledge that God doesn't let go of us. If we need confirmation of this we can take a look at Paul's second letter to Timothy (2 Tim. 2.11–13):

> Here is a trustworthy saying:
> If we died with him,
> we will also live with him;
> if we endure,
> we will also reign with him.
> If we disown him,
> he will also disown us;
> If we are faithless,
> he remains faithful,
> for he cannot disown himself.

Matthew 13.3–9, 18–23

> Then he told them many things in parables, saying: 'A farmer went out to sow his seed. As he was scattering the seed, some fell along the path, and the birds came and ate it up. Some fell on rocky places, where it did not have much soil. It sprang up quickly, because the soil was shallow. But when the sun came up, the plants were scorched, and they withered because they had no root. Other seed fell among thorns, which grew up and choked the plants. Still other seed fell on good soil, where it

produced a crop – a hundred, sixty or thirty times what was sown. Whoever has ears, let them hear.'

. . . 'Listen then to what the parable of the sower means: when anyone hears the message about the kingdom and does not understand it, the evil one comes and snatches away what was sown in their heart. This is the seed sown along the path. The seed falling on rocky ground refers to someone who hears the word and at once receives it with joy. But since they have no root, they last only a short time. When trouble or persecution comes because of the word, they quickly fall away. The seed falling among the thorns refers to someone who hears the word, but the worries of this life and the deceitfulness of wealth choke the word, making it unfruitful. But the seed falling on good soil refers to someone who hears the word and understands it. This is the one who produces a crop, yielding a hundred, sixty or thirty times what was sown.'

Day 23
Perseverance

Some say faith is a crutch,
to make an easier life for oneself;
a way to avoid facing difficulties by living in denial and
    calling it faith.
On the other hand,
some Christians think
once you know Jesus you're bullet-proof,
in the special club
where nothing can hurt or harm you.

None of the above reasoning is true. Having faith in God means we face the same life challenges as everyone else. The difference when we are walking with Jesus is that we have a totally different focus that undergirds and surrounds us.

- An eternal perspective means we see life beyond the time we are here in the flesh; our years here are the prologue.
- God is always at work in us; in everything there is something to learn, something to grow through, however painful that may be.
- Prayer changes things – the power of prayer can shift and change things miraculously.
- We are never alone – those feelings of isolation that so often accompany tribulation are met with the Holy Spirit, who is also known as 'the Comforter'.
- God hates injustice, so we can trust him with our complaints.
- He brings joy, even in times of trouble – a deep-seated sense of satisfaction that comes from knowing he cares and has our backs.

- There is always hope in God. Though we mourn and struggle, hope springs up. His hope lives in us and this hope can be experienced.

I could go on.

When we find ourselves at the bottom of a very dark pit, lost and fighting, he is always with us; he never leaves us or lets go. And in that place, as we reach out to find a path, we find gold. Gold that will shape our character and bring a harvest of maturity and a gift we can pass on to others. As we cry out for change, God shapes our prayers into, 'Change my circumstances or change me.'

Stay level minded and aware. The enemy of our souls is looking to catch us out, so remain alert. The suffering is for a season and is felt by all believers. Stay strong in the faith. In a while, God, who has great plans for our lives, will bring us into a new season. God knows what he is doing.

This is perseverance that bears fruit.

John 16.33b

In this world you will have trouble. But take heart! I have overcome the world.

2 Corinthians 4.8–9

We are hard pressed on every side, but not crushed; perplexed, but not in despair; persecuted, but not abandoned; struck down, but not destroyed.

James 1.2–4

Consider it pure joy, my brothers and sisters, whenever you face trials of many kinds, because you know that the testing of your faith produces perseverance. Let perseverance finish its work so that you may be mature and complete, not lacking anything.

Day 24
Abundant life

The Bible says that Jesus has come to give us everything in abundance, more than we expect – full life, filled to overflowing. This is a huge promise, but what does it really mean to live an abundant, overflowing life, and how do we get one?

This is where some Christians have stumbled by turning the scripture into a doctrine about financial prosperity or a 'Jesus is my jackpot' theology. Abundance is way deeper than simple outward showings of success or prosperity.

Life will bring us all kinds of challenges and all kinds of blessings, but as we walk with Jesus our lives begin to defy the typically expected responses. We become humble in blessing and hopeful in hardship. His peace transcends all understanding. His love, which the Bible says is so endless it's beyond knowing, anchors us. Every fibre of our thinking and being is filled to overflowing with his nature, his hope, his compassion, his truth, his joy, his love, his grace. This experience transforms us and means we see and experience the world through new eyes.

We find ourselves hopeful when there is little evidence for it. We take any blessing of status and use it to serve others. We find any good that is there to find, whatever the circumstances.

Not only this, in the good times there is also the concept of there being 'more than enough'. It is this 'more than enough' part that is for others, for giving, for serving, for sharing. When we experience this new way of looking at the world, it can often mean we hurt for and care for the world around us more too. The desire to reach out and relate to the world in a more meaningful way may increase.

When our desires are met in Jesus, everything else positions itself around this premier relationship. When we realize how deeply we are loved, how highly we are valued, and that our lives are uniquely infused with purpose, we can feel more satisfied, less desperate, more at one with the world and with ourselves.

The Bible tells us that God is able to do exceedingly abundantly above all that we ask or think, and he does it by his power, which is at work in us.

This scripture from 1 Corinthians 2.9 is definitely one to dwell on:

'What no eye has seen,
what no ear has heard,
and what no mind has conceived' –
the things God has prepared for those who love him.

John 10.10 (TPT)

Abundant life

A thief has only one thing in mind – he wants to steal, slaughter, and destroy. But I have come to *give you everything in abundance, more than you expect* – life in its fullness until you overflow!

Day 25
Behaviour

When considering this subject, it's essential to understand one thing: we are not loved more if our behaviour is exemplary, and we are not loved less if it's not. This has to be stated because to some people the word 'Christian' is a substitute for 'good person'.

In reality, a Christian is someone who has entered into relationship with Jesus, not someone who is necessarily a 'good person'. Some people are naturally more helpful, thoughtful, giving and generous than others. This natural kindness can be more to do with nature and nurture than faith. So 'Christian' and 'good person' aren't the same thing.

God loves us whether we are considered good or bad in our own and in other people's eyes. He loves us whatever our reputation and whatever our past, present or future actions. He loves us because *he is* love.

We didn't earn his love; we always had it, and we can't lose it.

Christian behaviour can be summed up in one word: *love*. *Love* God, *love* ourselves, *love* others. No judgement, no ego, just *love*. Now, it may sound difficult to love like this, but the great news is that we don't have to somehow create this love – God pours it into us. The journey into this love is progressive; we grow and change gradually over time, from the inside out.

Because of the love God pours into us, we grow in our love for ourselves and for others and for the world around us. How does God do this?

Well, people very rarely act out of character; we all act out of who we believe ourselves to be.

As we become more and more aware and welcoming of God's presence in our lives, we change. Who we consider ourselves to be and what we consider ourselves to be worth are challenged by how loved we are by God. Not loved because of what we do, but loved just for who we really are. We don't change so we can be loved more; rather, we are changed as we grow in recognizing and living in God's amazing love for us. Our behaviour and attitudes become outward presentations of progressive inner change. The Bible calls this 'fruit', and fruit doesn't magically appear; it grows. As we grow in depth with God, what people read as behaviour – kindness, love, humility, patience and so on – will naturally grow. So we can relax in the confidence that the more we get to know God, the more our decision-making, thought processes and actions will reflect him.

Romans 12.9–21 (MSG)

Love outworking

Love from the center of who you are; don't fake it. Run for dear life from evil; hold on for dear life to good. Be good friends who love deeply; practice playing second fiddle.

Don't burn out; keep yourselves fueled and aflame. Be alert servants of the Master, cheerfully expectant. Don't quit in hard times; pray all the harder. Help needy Christians; be inventive in hospitality.

Bless your enemies; no cursing under your breath. Laugh with your happy friends when they're happy; share tears when they're down. Get along with each other; don't be stuck-up. Make friends with nobodies; don't be the great somebody.

Don't hit back; discover beauty in everyone. If you've got it in you, get along with everybody. Don't insist on getting even; that's not for you to do. 'I'll do the judging,' says God. 'I'll take care of it.'

Day 25

Our Scriptures tell us that if you see your enemy hungry, go buy that person lunch, or if he's thirsty, get him a drink. Your generosity will surprise him with goodness. Don't let evil get the best of you; get the best of evil by doing good.

Day 26
Vulnerability

We live in a culture where it's difficult to be vulnerable. There is a pressure to achieve, to look good and to have it all together. When we make mistakes, or our lives look a little less than perfect, many of us don't dare to share our failings for fear of being shamed. As a result, we are far more likely to make the same mistakes again.

Some people feel desperately lonely but still present an image on social media of a singularly positive life – the 'humble brag', the 'quirky joke', the 'life is amazing' posts. And yet we see a striking rise in the number of people talking to professionals about having challenges with their mental health. It's hard for us to wholeheartedly be ourselves if we feel a constant sense of judgement.

When we are vulnerable, we cannot guarantee a positive response from others, so the best place to start our journey into vulnerability is with God, trusting him with all we are. There is a saying, 'You can't kill a dead man.' This means you cannot kill me if I am already dead! The Bible says we are dead in Christ. If this is the case, then we can be emboldened to be our true, warts-and-all selves with God and, in turn, with others.

The positive outcome of becoming vulnerable with God is that it can help us enter into a frame of thinking that enables us to lean in and to hear, sense and touch what God wants to reveal to us.

Another place we can experience feelings of extreme vulnerability is when we let go of control. The more we understand that God is trustworthy, the easier it becomes to put our trust in him day to day. The second part of Colossians 3.3 says that our lives are 'hidden with Christ'. As we experience this truth, we begin to reflect a more vulnerable side to the outside world. We begin to care less about what the world thinks because we know our lot is secure in God.

John 12.24

Death produces life

Very truly I tell you, unless a grain of wheat falls to the ground and dies, it remains only a single seed. But if it dies, it produces many seeds.

Day 27
Healing

The question is often asked, 'If God loves the world so much, why is there so much pain and suffering?' The next question might be, 'If he heals, why doesn't he heal everyone?'

The difficult truth is that while we are here on earth, we will never know why God heals one and not another. For those who do experience healing (and it does happen), every healing is unique: how it happens, when and why. Some experience it immediately and can see or feel a change in their mind or body straight away; for others it may take years, or they may experience a partial healing. Throughout this, we need to remember to ask God that his will be done and to keep our focus on the healer, not on the healing. This can be difficult as we wait for answers, but there is often healing in the waiting, with positive transformation to be experienced in many other ways.

We should not be focused solely on the result, although that is what we want, but the focus should be on the person of Jesus and the journey that he has us on. When we read about a healing in the Bible, the people have been looking for a way out of their suffering, and when they see or hear Jesus they may not understand everything about him, but they know he is the answer. From this we can see that healing is about reaching out to him, being bold to ask for a positive response and being mature in accepting his answer.

There is power in the name of Jesus to heal the sick and redeem the irredeemable. We can ask God for healing in the name of Jesus. God wants us to seek him, he wants us to have faith in him and he wants us to trust him with our hearts, minds, bodies and lives. There are many stories of people who have been healed in our times, so we know healings were not just for biblical times. We can dare to ask him, knowing he is both willing and able.

Having a life-long incurable disease can bring a challenge to our faith if nothing changes. There are no easy answers. It's a road we walk and evolve through. Aside from our own choices, we don't get to choose our challenges, but we can experience immense breakthrough in how we handle them and how God moves through them.

There are also different experiences of healing in different parts of the world, so clearly there is still a lot more to be understood and sought after in this area.

Sometimes people believe (or are told) they have not been healed because they are doing something wrong or because they aren't doing something they should be doing. Don't allow this type of thinking to poison your natural, trusting, faith-based relationship with God. Keep your focus on him. He started your journey and he will complete your journey.

Sometimes we experience total healing and sometimes we don't, but through it all, God never stops loving us, he never forgets us and he still has a purpose and plan for our lives.

Mark 5.25–34 (MSG)

Jesus heals the sick

A woman who had suffered a condition of hemorrhaging for twelve years – a long succession of physicians had treated her, and treated her badly, taking all her money and leaving her worse off than before – had heard about Jesus. She slipped in from behind and touched his robe. She was thinking to herself, 'If I can put a finger on his robe, I can get well.' The moment she did it, the flow of blood dried up. She could feel the change and knew her plague was over and done with.

At the same moment, Jesus felt energy discharging from him. He turned around to the crowd and asked, 'Who touched my robe?'

His disciples said, 'What are you talking about? With this crowd pushing and jostling you, you're asking, "Who touched me?" Dozens have touched you!'

But he went on asking, looking around to see who had done it. The woman, knowing what had happened, knowing she was the one, stepped up in fear and trembling, knelt before him, and gave him the whole story.

Jesus said to her, 'Daughter, you took a risk of faith, and now you're healed and whole. Live well, live blessed! Be healed of your plague.'

Day 28

Purpose and calling

Who am I? What am I here for? What's the point of me?

These are all questions we may have asked ourselves. When we walk with God and look at who he is, we begin to reflect him, and this is when we find out who we are. Once we know who we are, it becomes clearer what we are meant to do in life. Society gives recognition to special people with special callings, but actually everyone has a purpose and calling.

Some of the most purpose-driven people are those who have no money, no status, no apparent special skill, and yet it's as though they usher in the presence of God wherever they go. Their call is simply to 'be'. They make a positive change to people, places and situations just by their presence. Some people's skills and talents are hidden; some are super-exposed and on show for the world to see. This diversity is a wonderful thing; everyone gets to take part because everyone has something to offer.

One of the skills of a parent is to discover what their child is interested in, without prejudice, and to encourage that interest. As we find our interests, we often find our life's purpose. And when we walk alongside Jesus, he prompts us towards skills, talents, interests and certain people groups. As we begin to care about the lives of those around us, it becomes impossible not to engage. People who have led pretty average lives can find themselves emboldened to do things and to go to places they never would have dreamt of.

When we are young, we often dream of what we would like to do, but many of us will find ourselves using our second or third gift as our main occupation. Many of us bury our dreams and move on. We have let go of something we really loved. God often wants to restore those dreams to us. They may not be in the shape we first thought of, but they are nevertheless brought back to life in him in some way, shape or form.

Life experiences can also shape what we focus on. Some of these experiences may not be good ones, but God draws everything together for good, giving our life meaning and legacy.

The Bible says that when we 'cast [our] bread upon the waters' (Eccles. 11.1 ESV UK), it will not return void, meaning that when we sow, we will reap, and when we plant in faith, he brings harvest. We bear fruit, and this fruit is good for the picking and it is nourishing to eat. In the abundant life, the gifts we have multiply and have purpose.

Jeremiah 29.11–13

'For I know the plans I have for you,' declares the LORD, 'plans to prosper you and not to harm you, plans to give you hope and a future. Then you will call on me and come and pray to me, and I will listen to you. You will seek me and find me when you seek me with all your heart.'

Day 29

Gathering community

Many people, when they hear the words 'Christian community', think of monasteries or convents. In fact, the Bible describes Christian communities as the church, which is any gathering or collection of believers anywhere. So this thing we call 'church' isn't a building of bricks and mortar; instead, it's a building of hearts and minds. The church isn't the structure; it's the people in it. When you come into relationship with Jesus, you become part of his church.

We are encouraged to gather, to strengthen one another. Church should be a place where we are able to chew over issues of faith and ask *big* questions without fear of judgement. Where we can meet with others who help connect us more closely to God. This is often called **Fellowship**.

Church should be a place where we are able to speak to God and hear God collectively. Where we can, if we wish, be loud and expressive, or contemplative and reflective. This is often called **Worship**.

Church should be a place to discover together God's purpose for us, as individuals and as a collective. A place of envisioning and equipping us to be all God is calling us to be. This is often called **Mission**.

And it should be a place to encourage and pray for each other and to walk life-miles together. This is often called **Ministry**.

It should also be the perfect place to focus on Jesus and to show God's love to one another. In doing so, we strengthen each other to walk even more closely with Jesus. This is often called **Discipleship**.

There are also, surprisingly, health benefits from going to church. A survey of nearly 37,000 people shows that people attending church more regularly are likely to experience less depression.[5]

According to the findings of another study, there is a serious correlation between church attendance and better sleep.[6]

It seems that when we make gathering in Christian community an integral part of our lives, we not only improve our relationship with God, but we are also strengthened, and we improve our relationships with those around us.

Can you be a Christian and not go to church? Yes, you can, but in the words of an old proverb, 'If you want to go fast, go alone. If you want to go far, go with others.'

Hebrews 10.24–25

And let us consider how we may spur one another on towards love and good deeds, not giving up meeting together, as some are in the habit of doing, but encouraging one another – and all the more as you see the Day approaching.

Day 30
Curiosity

Curiosity is essential to growth.

Jesus *was asked* 183 questions.

Jesus *asked* more than 300 questions.

He modelled searching, enquiring, questioning, talking and seeking. And he encouraged us to ask, to seek and to knock. In other words, be curious, be enquiring, be open.

If we stop being these things, we can end up stuck in a box. Boxes can be constricting, but exploration of faith and the Bible should be encouraged without fear.

- We are on shaky ground when we insist that our world view is the only right world view and that anything contradicting that view is wrong. If all deviation is seen as threatening, we cannot explore and investigate together; it leaves no room for movement. Remain curious.
- Insisting that things remain the same and that change cannot occur is dangerous, especially if we apply this to areas such as culture, style and identity. Change is good.
- Rigid conformity demands that we must not stand out. The 'Who do you think you are?' 'What makes *you* so special?' attitude can kill our confidence and any belief in the uniqueness of our identity. Be your unique self.
- If we refuse to entertain questions and then insist that questioning is rebellious, we are using our power to control others. The judgement and condemnation that rains down on an innocent enquirer is often awful to watch. It's also interesting to observe the rage in the hearts of the corrector. Sadly, we see it

everywhere on social media. Rage. Boxed-in thinking requires a degree of rage to survive. Questions lead to growth.

- Black-and-white thinking produces simplistic thinking: the goodies and the baddies – which side are you on? Our faith is so much bigger than this. Grey is OK.
- Often the above points are held in place by fear – messages that there will be catastrophic consequences to our lives if we do not follow the majority, whoever they are, in any given situation. Do not be afraid.
- And to finish it off is the lock and key of the box: shame. If we can't get past shame, we'll never get out. It's the lynchpin that holds everything in place. Shame has no place in the life of grace.

We are better than the box.

As you discover God's love, you'll find more and more that questions are welcome. If you are looking for a community to share your faith with, make sure it's one where questions are welcome. God answers questions, gives certainty, offers security. Ask and keep asking. Knock and keep knocking. Search and keep searching.

Life-changing answers are responses to life-changing questions. Seek the questions. Break out of the box. Stay curious.

Matthew 7.7

Ask and it will be given to you; seek and you will find; knock and the door will be opened to you.

Daily reading plan:
the Gospel of Mark

Day 1	Mark 1.1–20
Day 2	Mark 1.21–45
Day 3	Mark 2.1–17
Day 4	Mark 2.18–28
Day 5	Mark 3.1–19
Day 6	Mark 3.20–35
Day 7	Mark 4.1–20
Day 8	Mark 4.21–41
Day 9	Mark 5.1–20
Day 10	Mark 5.21–43
Day 11	Mark 6.1–29
Day 12	Mark 6.30–56
Day 13	Mark 7.1–23
Day 14	Mark 7.24–37
Day 15	Mark 8.1–21
Day 16	Mark 8.22–38
Day 17	Mark 9.1–32
Day 18	Mark 9.33–50
Day 19	Mark 10.1–31
Day 20	Mark 10.32–52
Day 21	Mark 11.1–33
Day 22	Mark 12.1–27
Day 23	Mark 12.28–44
Day 24	Mark 13.1–37
Day 25	Mark 14.1–11
Day 26	Mark 14.12–31
Day 27	Mark 14.32–72

The Gospel of Mark

John the Baptist prepares the way

1 This is the Good News about Jesus the Messiah, the Son of God.*ᵃ* It began ²just as the prophet Isaiah had written:

'Look, I am sending my messenger ahead of you,
    and he will prepare your way.*ᵇ*
³He is a voice shouting in the wilderness,
"Prepare the way for the Lord's coming!
    Clear the road for him!"*ᶜ*'

⁴This messenger was John the Baptist. He was in the wilderness and preached that people should be baptized to show that they had repented of their sins and turned to God to be forgiven. ⁵All of Judea, including all the people of Jerusalem, went out to see and hear John. And when they confessed their sins, he baptized them in the River Jordan. ⁶His clothes were woven from coarse camel hair, and he wore a leather belt around his waist. For food he ate locusts and wild honey.

⁷John announced: 'Someone is coming soon who is greater than I am – so much greater that I'm not even worthy to stoop down like a slave and untie the straps of his sandals. ⁸I baptize you with*ᵈ* water, but he will baptize you with the Holy Spirit!'

---

a Some manuscripts do not include *the Son of God*.

b Mal 3:1.

c Isa 40:3 (Greek version).

d Or *in*; also in 1:8b.

The baptism and temptation of Jesus

[9]One day Jesus came from Nazareth in Galilee, and John baptized him in the River Jordan. [10]As Jesus came up out of the water, he saw the heavens splitting apart and the Holy Spirit descending on him[e] like a dove. [11]And a voice from heaven said, 'You are my dearly loved Son, and you bring me great joy.'

[12]The Spirit then compelled Jesus to go into the wilderness, [13]where he was tempted by Satan for forty days. He was out among the wild animals, and angels took care of him.

[14]Later on, after John was arrested, Jesus went into Galilee, where he preached God's Good News.[f] [15]'The time promised by God has come at last!' he announced. 'The Kingdom of God is near! Repent of your sins and believe the Good News!'

The first disciples

[16]One day as Jesus was walking along the shore of the Sea of Galilee, he saw Simon[g] and his brother Andrew throwing a net into the water, for they fished for a living. [17]Jesus called out to them, 'Come, follow me, and I will show you how to fish for people!' [18]And they left their nets at once and followed him.

[19]A little farther up the shore Jesus saw Zebedee's sons, James and John, in a boat repairing their nets. [20]He called them at once, and they also followed him, leaving their father, Zebedee, in the boat with the hired men.

Jesus casts out an evil spirit

[21]Jesus and his companions went to the town of Capernaum. When the Sabbath day came, he went into the synagogue and began to teach. [22]The people were amazed at his teaching, for he taught with real authority – quite unlike the teachers of religious law.

---

e   Or *towards him,* or *into him.*

f   Some manuscripts read *the Good News of the Kingdom of God.*

g   *Simon* is called 'Peter' in 3:16 and thereafter.

[23]Suddenly, a man in the synagogue who was possessed by an evil[h] spirit cried out, [24]'Why are you interfering with us, Jesus of Nazareth? Have you come to destroy us? I know who you are – the Holy One of God!'

[25]But Jesus reprimanded him. 'Be quiet! Come out of the man,' he ordered. [26]At that, the evil spirit screamed, threw the man into a convulsion, and then came out of him.

[27]Amazement gripped the audience, and they began to discuss what had happened. 'What sort of new teaching is this?' they asked excitedly. 'It has such authority! Even evil spirits obey his orders!' [28]The news about Jesus spread quickly throughout the entire region of Galilee.

Jesus heals many people

[29]After Jesus left the synagogue with James and John, they went to Simon and Andrew's home. [30]Now Simon's mother-in-law was sick in bed with a high fever. They told Jesus about her right away. [31]So he went to her bedside, took her by the hand, and helped her sit up. Then the fever left her, and she prepared a meal for them.

[32]That evening after sunset, many sick and demon-possessed people were brought to Jesus. [33]The whole town gathered at the door to watch. [34]So Jesus healed many people who were sick with various diseases, and he cast out many demons. But because the demons knew who he was, he did not allow them to speak.

Jesus preaches in Galilee

[35]Before daybreak the next morning, Jesus got up and went out to an isolated place to pray. [36]Later Simon and the others went out to find him. [37]When they found him, they said, 'Everyone is looking for you.'

---

h   Greek *unclean;* also in 1:26, 27.

[38]But Jesus replied, 'We must go on to other towns as well, and I will preach to them, too. That is why I came.' [39]So he travelled throughout the region of Galilee, preaching in the synagogues and casting out demons.

Jesus heals a man with leprosy

[40]A man with leprosy came and knelt in front of Jesus, begging to be healed. 'If you are willing, you can heal me and make me clean,' he said.

[41]Moved with compassion,[i] Jesus reached out and touched him. 'I am willing,' he said. 'Be healed!' [42]Instantly the leprosy disappeared, and the man was healed. [43]Then Jesus sent him on his way with a stern warning: [44]'Don't tell anyone about this. Instead, go to the priest and let him examine you. Take along the offering required in the law of Moses for those who have been healed of leprosy.[j] This will be a public testimony that you have been cleansed.'

[45]But the man went and spread the word, proclaiming to everyone what had happened. As a result, large crowds soon surrounded Jesus, and he couldn't publicly enter a town anywhere. He had to stay out in the secluded places, but people from everywhere kept coming to him.

Jesus heals a paralysed man

2 When Jesus returned to Capernaum several days later, the news spread quickly that he was back home. [2]Soon the house where he was staying was so packed with visitors that there was no more room, even outside the door. While he was preaching God's word to them, [3]four men arrived carrying a paralysed man on a mat. [4]They couldn't bring him to Jesus because of the crowd, so they dug a hole through the roof above his head. Then they lowered the man on his mat, right

---

i   Some manuscripts read *Moved with anger.*

j   See Lev 14:2-32.

down in front of Jesus. [5]Seeing their faith, Jesus said to the paralysed man, 'My child, your sins are forgiven.'

[6]But some of the teachers of religious law who were sitting there thought to themselves, [7]'What is he saying? This is blasphemy! Only God can forgive sins!'

[8]Jesus knew immediately what they were thinking, so he asked them, 'Why do you question this in your hearts? [9]Is it easier to say to the paralysed man "Your sins are forgiven", or "Stand up, pick up your mat, and walk"? [10]So I will prove to you that the Son of Man[a] has the authority on earth to forgive sins.' Then Jesus turned to the paralysed man and said, [11]'Stand up, pick up your mat, and go home!'

[12]And the man jumped up, grabbed his mat, and walked out through the stunned onlookers. They were all amazed and praised God, exclaiming, 'We've never seen anything like this before!'

Jesus calls Levi (Matthew)

[13]Then Jesus went out to the lakeside again and taught the crowds that were coming to him. [14]As he walked along, he saw Levi son of Alphaeus sitting at his tax collector's booth. 'Follow me and be my disciple,' Jesus said to him. So Levi got up and followed him.

[15]Later, Levi invited Jesus and his disciples to his home as dinner guests, along with many tax collectors and other disreputable sinners. (There were many people of this kind among Jesus' followers.) [16]But when the teachers of religious law who were Pharisees[b] saw him eating with tax collectors and other sinners, they asked his disciples, 'Why does he eat with such scum?[c]'

[17]When Jesus heard this, he told them, 'Healthy people don't need a doctor – sick people do. I have come to call not those who think they are righteous, but those who know they are sinners.'

---

a 'Son of Man' is a title Jesus used for himself.

b Greek *the scribes of the Pharisees.*

c Greek *with tax collectors and sinners?*

A discussion about fasting

[18]Once when John's disciples and the Pharisees were fasting, some people came to Jesus and asked, 'Why don't your disciples fast as John's disciples and the Pharisees do?'

[19]Jesus replied, 'Do wedding guests fast while celebrating with the groom? Of course not. They can't fast while the groom is with them. [20]But some day the groom will be taken away from them, and then they will fast.

[21]'Besides, who would patch old clothing with new cloth? For the new patch would shrink and rip away from the old cloth, leaving an even bigger tear than before.

[22]'And no one puts new wine into old wine skins. For the wine would burst the wine skins, and the wine and the skins would both be lost. New wine calls for new wineskins.'

A discussion about the Sabbath

[23]One Sabbath day as Jesus was walking through some grainfields, his disciples began breaking of heads of grain to eat. [24]But the Pharisees said to Jesus, 'Look, why are they breaking the law by harvesting grain on the Sabbath?'

[25]Jesus said to them, 'Haven't you ever read in the Scriptures what David did when he and his companions were hungry? [26]He went into the house of God (during the days when Abiathar was high priest) and broke the law by eating the sacred loaves of bread that only the priests are allowed to eat. He also gave some to his companions.'

[27]Then Jesus said to them, 'The Sab bath was made to meet the needs of people, and not people to meet the requirements of the Sabbath. [28]So the Son of Man is Lord, even over the Sabbath!'

Jesus heals on the Sabbath

3 Jesus went into the synagogue again and noticed a man with a deformed hand. [2]Since it was the Sab bath, Jesus' enemies watched him closely. If he healed the man's hand, they planned to accuse him of working on the Sabbath.

³Jesus said to the man with the deformed hand, 'Come and stand in front of everyone.' ⁴Then he turned to his critics and asked, 'Does the law permit good deeds on the Sabbath, or is it a day for doing evil? Is this a day to save life or to destroy it?' But they wouldn't answer him.

⁵He looked around at them angrily and was deeply saddened by their hard hearts. Then he said to the man, 'Hold out your hand.' So the man held out his hand, and it was restored! ⁶At once the Pharisees went away and met with the supporters of Herod to plot how to kill Jesus.

Crowds follow Jesus

⁷Jesus went out to the lake with his disciples, and a large crowd followed him. They came from all over Galilee, Judea, ⁸Jerusalem, Idumea, from east of the River Jordan, and even from as far north as Tyre and Sidon. The news about his miracles had spread far and wide, and vast numbers of people came to see him.

⁹Jesus instructed his disciples to have a boat ready so the crowd would not crush him. ¹⁰He had healed many people that day, so all the sick people eagerly pushed forward to touch him. ¹¹And whenever those possessed by evil*d* spirits caught sight of him, the spirits would throw them to the ground in front of him shrieking, 'You are the Son of God!' ¹²But Jesus sternly commanded the spirits not to reveal who he was.

Jesus chooses the twelve apostles

¹³Afterwards Jesus went up on a mountain and called out the ones he wanted to go with him. And they came to him. ¹⁴Then he appointed twelve of them and called them his apostles.*e* They were to

---

d Greek *unclean;* also in 3:30.

e Some manuscripts do not include *and called them his apostles.*

accompany him, and he would send them out to preach, [15]giving them authority to cast out demons. [16]These are the twelve he chose:

> Simon (whom he named Peter),
> [17]James and John (the sons of Zebedee,
> but Jesus nicknamed them 'Sons of Thunder'[f]),
> [18]Andrew,
> Philip,
> Bartholomew, Matthew, Thomas,
> James (son of Alphaeus),
> Thaddaeus,
> Simon (the zealot[g]),
> [19]Judas Iscariot (who later betrayed him).

Jesus and the prince of demons

[20]On one occasion Jesus entered a house, and the crowds began to gather again. Soon he and his disciples couldn't even find time to eat. [21]When his family heard what was happening, they tried to take him away. 'He's out of his mind,' they said.

[22]But the teachers of religious law who had arrived from Jerusalem said, 'He's possessed by Satan,[h] the prince of demons. That's where he gets the power to cast out demons.'

[23]Jesus called them over and responded with an illustration. 'How can Satan cast out Satan?' he asked. [24]'A kingdom divided by civil war will collapse. [25]Similarly, a family splintered by feuding will fall apart. [26]And if Satan is divided and fights against himself, how can he stand? He would never survive. [27]Let me illustrate this further. Who is powerful enough to enter the house of a strong man and

---

f   Greek *whom he named Boanerges, which means Sons of Thunder.*

g   Greek *the Cananean,* an Aramaic term for Jewish nationalists.

h   Greek *Beelzeboul;* other manuscripts read *Beezeboul;* Latin version reads *Beelzebub.*

plunder his goods? Only someone even stronger – someone who could tie him up and then plunder his house.

²⁸'I tell you the truth, all sin and blasphemy can be forgiven, ²⁹but anyone who blasphemes the Holy Spirit will never be forgiven. This is a sin with eternal consequences.' ³⁰He told them this because they were saying, 'He's possessed by an evil spirit.'

The true family of Jesus

³¹Then Jesus' mother and brothers came to see him. They stood out-side and sent word for him to come out and talk with them. ³²There was a crowd sitting around Jesus, and someone said, 'Your mother and your brothers[a] are outside asking for you.'

³³Jesus replied, 'Who is my mother? Who are my brothers?' ³⁴Then he looked at those around him and said, 'Look, these are my mother and brothers. ³⁵Anyone who does God's will is my brother and sister and mother.'

Parable of the farmer scattering seed

4 Once again Jesus began teaching by the lakeside. A very large crowd soon gathered around him, so he got into a boat. Then he sat in the boat while all the people remained on the shore. ²He taught them by telling many stories in the form of parables, such as this one:

³'Listen! A farmer went out to plant some seed. ⁴As he scattered it across his field, some of the seed fell on a footpath, and the birds came and ate it. ⁵Other seed fell on shallow soil with underlying rock. The seed sprouted quickly because the soil was shallow. ⁶But the plant soon wilted under the hot sun, and since it didn't have deep roots, it died. ⁷Other seed fell among thorns that grew up and choked out the tender plants so they produced no grain. ⁸Still other seeds fell on fertile soil, and they sprouted, grew, and produced a crop that

---

a   Some manuscripts add *and sisters*.

was thirty, sixty, and even a hundred times as much as had been planted!' ⁹Then he said, 'Anyone with ears to hear should listen and understand.'

¹⁰Later, when Jesus was alone with the twelve disciples and with the others who were gathered around, they asked him what the parables meant.

¹¹He replied, 'You are permitted to understand the secret[b] of the Kingdom of God. But I use parables for everything I say to outsiders, ¹²so that the Scriptures might be fulfilled:

"When they see what I do,
    they will learn nothing.
When they hear what I say,
    they will not understand.
Otherwise, they will turn to me
    and be forgiven."[c]'

¹³Then Jesus said to them, 'If you can't understand the meaning of this parable, how will you understand all the other parables? ¹⁴The farmer plants seed by taking God's word to others. ¹⁵The seed that fell on the footpath represents those who hear the message, only to have Satan come at once and take it away. ¹⁶The seed on the rocky soil represents those who hear the message and immediately receive it with joy. ¹⁷But since they don't have deep roots, they don't last long. They fall away as soon as they have problems or are persecuted for believing God's word. ¹⁸The seed that fell among the thorns represents others who hear God's word, ¹⁹but all too quickly the message is crowded out by the worries of this life, the lure of wealth, and the desire for other things, so no fruit is produced. ²⁰And the seed that fell on good soil represents those who hear and accept God's word

---

b   Greek *mystery*.

c   Isa 6:9-10 (Greek version).

and produce a harvest of thirty, sixty, or even a hundred times as much as had been planted!'

Parable of the lamp

[21]Then Jesus asked them, 'Would anyone light a lamp and then put it under a basket or under a bed? Of course not! A lamp is placed on a stand, where its light will shine. [22]For everything that is hidden will eventually be brought into the open, and every secret will be brought to light. [23]Anyone with ears to hear should listen and understand.'

[24]Then he added, 'Pay close attention to what you hear. The closer you listen, the more understanding you will be given[d] – and you will receive even more. [25]To those who listen to my teaching, more understanding will be given. But for those who are not listening, even what little understanding they have will be taken away from them.'

Parable of the growing seed

[26]Jesus also said, 'The Kingdom of God is like a farmer who scatters seed on the ground. [27]Night and day, while he's asleep or awake, the seed sprouts and grows, but he does not understand how it happens. [28]The earth produces the crops on its own. First a leaf blade pushes through, then the heads of wheat are formed, and finally the grain ripens. [29]And as soon as the grain is ready, the farmer comes and harvests it with a sickle, for the harvest time has come.'

Parable of the mustard seed

[30]Jesus said, 'How can I describe the Kingdom of God? What story should I use to illustrate it? [31]It is like a mustard seed planted in the ground. It is the smallest of all seeds, [32]but it becomes the largest of all garden plants; it grows long branches, and birds can make nests in its shade.'

---

d Or *The measure you give will be the measure you get back.*

[33]Jesus used many similar stories and illustrations to teach the people as much as they could understand. [34]In fact, in his public ministry he never taught without using parables; but afterwards, when he was alone with his disciples, he explained every thing to them.

Jesus calms the storm

[35]As evening came, Jesus said to his disciples, 'Let's cross to the other side of the lake.' [36]So they took Jesus in the boat and started out, leaving the crowds behind (although other boats followed). [37]But soon a fierce storm came up. High waves were breaking into the boat, and it began to fill with water.

[38]Jesus was sleeping at the back of the boat with his head on a cushion. The disciples woke him up, shouting, 'Teacher, don't you care that we're going to drown?'

[39]When Jesus woke up, he rebuked the wind and said to the waves, 'Silence! Be still!' Suddenly the wind stopped, and there was a great calm. [40]Then he asked them, 'Why are you afraid? Do you still have no faith?'

[41]The disciples were absolutely terrified. 'Who is this man?' they asked each other. 'Even the wind and waves obey him!'

Jesus heals a demon-possessed man

5 So they arrived at the other side of the lake, in the region of the Gerasenes.[e] [2]When Jesus climbed out of the boat, a man possessed by an evil[f] spirit came out from the tombs to meet him. [3]This man lived in the burial caves and could no longer be restrained, even with a chain. [4]Whenever he was put into chains and shackles – as he often was – he snapped the chains from his wrists and smashed the

---

e   Other manuscripts read *Gadarenes;* still others read *Gergesenes.* See Matt 8:28; Luke 8:26.

f   Greek *unclean;* also in 5:8, 13.

shackles. No one was strong enough to subdue him. [5]Day and night he wandered among the burial caves and in the hills, howling and cutting himself with sharp stones.

[6]When Jesus was still some distance away, the man saw him, ran to meet him, and bowed low before him. [7]With a shriek, he screamed, 'Why are you interfering with me, Jesus, Son of the Most High God? In the name of God, I beg you, don't torture me!' [8]For Jesus had already said to the spirit, 'Come out of the man, you evil spirit.'

[9]Then Jesus demanded, 'What is your name?'

And he replied, 'My name is Legion, because there are many of us inside this man.' [10]Then the evil spirits begged him again and again not to send them to some distant place.

[11]There happened to be a large herd of pigs feeding on the hillside nearby. [12]'Send us into those pigs,' the spirits begged. 'Let us enter them.'

[13]So Jesus gave them permission. The evil spirits came out of the man and entered the pigs, and the entire herd of about 2,000 pigs plunged down the steep hillside into the lake and drowned in the water.

[14]The herdsmen fled to the nearby town and the surrounding countryside, spreading the news as they ran. People rushed out to see what had happened. [15]A crowd soon gathered around Jesus, and they saw the man who had been possessed by the legion of demons. He was sitting there fully clothed and perfectly sane, and they were all afraid. [16]Then those who had seen what happened told the others about the demon-possessed man and the pigs. [17]And the crowd began pleading with Jesus to go away and leave them alone.

[18]As Jesus was getting into the boat, the man who had been demon possessed begged to go with him. [19]But Jesus said, 'No, go home to your family, and tell them everything the Lord has done for you and how merciful he has been.' [20]So the man started off to

visit the Ten Towns[a] of that region and began to proclaim the great things Jesus had done for him; and everyone was amazed at what he told them.

Jesus heals in response to faith

[21]Jesus got into the boat again and went back to the other side of the lake, where a large crowd gathered around him on the shore. [22]Then a leader of the local synagogue, whose name was Jairus, arrived. When he saw Jesus, he fell at his feet, [23]pleading fervently with him. 'My little daughter is dying,' he said. 'Please come and lay your hands on her; heal her so she can live.'

[24]Jesus went with him, and all the people followed, crowding around him. [25]A woman in the crowd had suffered for twelve years with constant bleeding. [26]She had suffered a great deal from many doctors, and over the years she had spent everything she had to pay them, but she got no better. In fact, she was worse. [27]She had heard about Jesus, so she came up behind him through the crowd and touched his robe. [28]For she thought to herself, 'If I can just touch his robe, I will be healed.' [29]Immediately the bleeding stopped, and she could feel in her body that she had been healed of her terrible condition.

[30]Jesus realized at once that healing power had gone out from him, so he turned around in the crowd and asked, 'Who touched my robe?'

[31]His disciples said to him, 'Look at this crowd pressing around you. How can you ask, "Who touched me?"'

[32]But he kept on looking around to see who had done it. [33]Then the frightened woman, trembling at the realization of what had happened to her, came and fell to her knees in front of him and told him what she had done. [34]And he said to her, 'Daughter, your faith has made you well. Go in peace. Your suffering is over.'

---

a   Greek *Decapolis*.

³⁵While he was still speaking to her, messengers arrived from the home of Jairus, the leader of the synagogue. They told him, 'Your daughter is dead. There's no use troubling the Teacher now.'

³⁶But Jesus overheard*ᵇ* them and said to Jairus, 'Don't be afraid. Just have faith.'

³⁷Then Jesus stopped the crowd and wouldn't let anyone go with him except Peter, James, and John (the brother of James). ³⁸When they came to the home of the synagogue leader, Jesus saw much commotion and weeping and wailing. ³⁹He went inside and asked, 'Why all this commotion and weeping? The child isn't dead; she's only asleep.'

⁴⁰The crowd laughed at him. But he made them all leave, and he took the girl's father and mother and his three disciples into the room where the girl was lying. ⁴¹Holding her hand, he said to her, *'Talitha koum,'* which means 'Little girl, get up!' ⁴²And the girl, who was twelve years old, immediately stood up and walked around! They were overwhelmed and totally amazed. ⁴³Jesus gave them strict orders not to tell anyone what had happened, and then he told them to give her something to eat.

Jesus rejected at Nazareth

6 Jesus left that part of the country and returned with his disciples to Nazareth, his home town. ²The next Sabbath he began teaching in the synagogue, and many who heard him were amazed. They asked, 'Where did he get all this wisdom and the power to perform such miracles?' ³Then they scoffed, 'He's just a carpenter, the son of Mary*ᶜ* and the brother of James, Joseph,*ᵈ* Judas, and Simon. And his sisters live right here among us.' They were deeply offended and refused to believe in him.

---

b Or *ignored.*

c Some manuscripts read *He's just the son of the carpenter and of Mary.*

d Most manuscripts read *Joses;* see Matt 13:55.

[4]Then Jesus told them, 'A prophet is honoured everywhere except in his own home town and among his relatives and his own family.' [5]And because of their unbelief, he couldn't do any miracles among them except to place his hands on a few sick people and heal them. [6]And he was amazed at their unbelief.

Jesus sends out the twelve disciples

Then Jesus went from village to village, teaching the people. [7]And he called his twelve disciples together and began sending them out two by two, giving them authority to cast out evil[e] spirits. [8]He told them to take nothing for their journey except a walking stick – no food, no traveller's bag, no money.[f] [9]He allowed them to wear sandals but not to take a change of clothes.

[10]'Wherever you go,' he said, 'stay in the same house until you leave town. [11] But if any place refuses to welcome you or listen to you, shake its dust from your feet as you leave to show that you have abandoned those people to their fate.'

[12]So the disciples went out, telling everyone they met to repent of their sins and turn to God. [13]And they cast out many demons and healed many sick people, anointing them with olive oil.

The death of John the Baptist

[14]Herod Antipas, the king, soon heard about Jesus, because everyone was talking about him. Some were saying,[g] 'This must be John the Baptist raised from the dead. That is why he can do such miracles.' [15]Others said, 'He's the prophet Elijah.' Still others said, 'He's a prophet like the other great prophets of the past.'

---

e Greek *unclean.*

f Greek *no copper coins in their money belts.*

g Some manuscripts read *He was saying.*

[16]When Herod heard about Jesus, he said, 'John, the man I beheaded, has come back from the dead.'

[17]For Herod had sent soldiers to arrest and imprison John as a favour to Herodias. She had been his brother Philip's wife, but Herod had married her. [18]John had been telling Herod, 'It is against God's law for you to marry your brother's wife.' [19] So Herodias bore a grudge against John and wanted to kill him. But without Herod's approval she was powerless, [20]for Herod respected John; and knowing that he was a good and holy man, he protected him. Herod was greatly disturbed whenever he talked with John, but even so, he liked to listen to him.

[21]Herodias's chance finally came on Herod's birthday. He gave a party for his high government officials, army officers, and the leading citizens of Galilee. [22]Then his daughter, also named Herodias,[a] came in and performed a dance that greatly pleased Herod and his guests. 'Ask me for anything you like,' the king said to the girl, 'and I will give it to you.' [23]He even vowed, 'I will give you whatever you ask, up to half my kingdom!'

[24]She went out and asked her mother, 'What should I ask for?'

Her mother told her, 'Ask for the head of John the Baptist!'

[25]So the girl hurried back to the king and told him, 'I want the head of John the Baptist, right now, on a tray!'

[26]Then the king deeply regretted what he had said; but because of the vows he had made in front of his guests, he couldn't refuse her. [27]So he immediately sent an executioner to the prison to cut of John's head and bring it to him. The soldier beheaded John in the prison, [28]brought his head on a tray, and gave it to the girl, who took it to her mother. [29]When John's disciples heard what had happened, they came to get his body and buried it in a tomb.

---

a Some manuscripts read *the daughter of Herodias herself.*

Jesus feeds five thousand

[30]The apostles returned to Jesus and told him all they had done and taught. [31]Then Jesus said, 'Let's go of by ourselves to a quiet place and rest a while.' He said this because there were so many people coming and going that Jesus and his apostles didn't even have time to eat.

[32]So they left by boat for a quiet place, where they could be alone. [33]But many people recognized them and saw them leaving, and people from many towns ran ahead along the shore and got there ahead of them. [34]Jesus saw the huge crowd as he stepped from the boat, and he had compassion on them because they were like sheep without a shepherd. So he began teaching them many things.

[35]Late in the afternoon his disciples came to him and said, 'This is a remote place, and it's already getting late. [36]Send the crowds away so they can go to the nearby farms and villages and buy something to eat.'

[37]But Jesus said, 'You feed them.'

'With what?' they asked. 'We'd have to work for months to earn enough money[b] to buy food for all these people!'

[38]'How much bread do you have?' he asked. 'Go and find out.'

They came back and reported, 'We have five loaves of bread and two fish.'

[39]Then Jesus told the disciples to have the people sit down in groups on the green grass. [40]So they sat down in groups of fifty or a hundred.

[41]Jesus took the five loaves and two fish, looked up towards heaven, and blessed them. Then, breaking the loaves into pieces, he kept giving the bread to the disciples so they could distribute it to the people. He also divided the fish for everyone to share. [42]They all ate as much as they wanted, [43]and afterwards, the disciples picked up

---

b   Greek *It would take 200 denarii.* A denarius was equivalent to a labourer's full day's wage.

twelve baskets of leftover bread and fish. [44]A total of 5,000 men and their families were fed.[c]

Jesus walks on water

[45]Immediately after this, Jesus insisted that his disciples get back into the boat and head across the lake to Bethsaida, while he sent the people home. [46]After saying goodbye, he went up into the hills by himself to pray.

[47]Late that night, the disciples were in their boat in the middle of the lake, and Jesus was alone on land. [48]He saw that they were in serious trouble, rowing hard and struggling against the wind and waves. About three o'clock in the morning[d] Jesus came towards them, walking on the water. He intended to go past them, [49]but when they saw him walking on the water, they cried out in terror, thinking he was a ghost. [50]They were all terrified when they saw him.

But Jesus spoke to them at once. 'Don't be afraid,' he said. 'Take courage! I am here!'[e] [51]Then he climbed into the boat, and the wind stopped. They were totally amazed, [52]for they still didn't understand the significance of the miracle of the loaves. Their hearts were too hard to take it in.

[53]After they had crossed the lake, they landed at Gennesaret. They brought the boat to shore [54]and climbed out. The people recognized Jesus at once, [55]and they ran throughout the whole area, carrying sick people on mats to wherever they heard he was. [56]Wherever he went – in villages, cities, or the countryside – they brought the sick out to the market-places. They begged him to let the sick touch at least the fringe of his robe, and all who touched him were healed.

---

c   Some manuscripts read *fed from the loaves*.

d   Greek *About the fourth watch of the night*.

e   Or *The "I am" is here*; Greek reads *I am*. See Exod 3:14.

Jesus teaches about inner purity

7 One day some Pharisees and teachers of religious law arrived from Jerusalem to see Jesus. ²They noticed that some of his disciples failed to follow the Jewish ritual of hand washing before eating. ³(The Jews, especially the Pharisees, do not eat until they have poured water over their cupped hands,*f* as required by their ancient traditions. ⁴Similarly, they don't eat anything from the market until they immerse their hands*g* in water. This is but one of many traditions they have clung to – such as their ceremonial washing of cups, jugs, and kettles*h*.)

⁵So the Pharisees and teachers of religious law asked him, 'Why don't your disciples follow our age-old tradition? They eat without first performing the hand-washing ceremony.'

⁶Jesus replied, 'You hypocrites! Isaiah was right when he prophesied about you, for he wrote,

> "These people honour me with their lips,
>   but their hearts are far from me.
> ⁷Their worship is a farce,
>   for they teach man-made ideas as commands from
>   God."*i*

⁸For you ignore God's law and substitute your own tradition.'

⁹Then he said, 'You skilfully sidestep God's law in order to hold on to your own tradition. ¹⁰For instance, Moses gave you this law from

---

f Greek *have washed with the first.*

g Some manuscripts read *sprinkle themselves.*

h Some manuscripts add *and dining couches.*

i Isa 29:13 (Greek version).

God: "Honour your father and mother,"[a] and "Anyone who speaks disrespectfully of father or mother must be put to death."[b] ¹¹But you say it is all right for people to say to their parents, "Sorry, I can't help you. For I have vowed to give to God what I would have given to you."[c] ¹²In this way, you let them disregard their needy parents. ¹³And so you cancel the word of God in order to hand down your own tradition. And this is only one example among many others.'

¹⁴Then Jesus called to the crowd to come and hear. 'All of you listen,' he said, 'and try to understand. ¹⁵It's not what goes into your body that defiles you; you are defiled by what comes from your heart.[d]'

¹⁷Then Jesus went into a house to get away from the crowd, and his disciples asked him what he meant by the parable he had just used. ¹⁸'Don't you understand either?' he asked. 'Can't you see that the food you put into your body cannot defile you? ¹⁹Food doesn't go into your heart, but only passes through the stomach and then comes out again.' (By saying this, he declared that every kind of food is acceptable in God's eyes.)

²⁰And then he added, 'It is what comes from inside that defiles you. ²¹For from within, out of a person's heart, come evil thoughts, sexual immorality, theft, murder, ²²adultery, greed, wickedness, deceit, lustful desires, envy, slander, pride, and foolishness. ²³All these vile things come from within; they are what defile you.'

The faith of a Gentile woman

²⁴Then Jesus left Galilee and went north to the region of Tyre.[e] He didn't want anyone to know which house he was staying in, but he couldn't keep it a secret. ²⁵Right away a woman who had heard about

---

a   Exod 20:12; Deut 5:16.

b   Exod 21:17 (Greek version); Lev 20:9 (Greek version).

c   Greek *"What I would have given to you is Corban" (that is, a gift).*

d   Some manuscripts add verse 16, *Anyone with ears to hear should listen and understand.* Compare 4:9, 23.

e   Some manuscripts add *and Sidon.*

him came and fell at his feet. Her little girl was possessed by an evil[f] spirit, [26]and she begged him to cast out the demon from her daughter.

Since she was a Gentile, born in Syrian Phoenicia, [27]Jesus told her, 'First I should feed the children – my own family, the Jews.[g] It isn't right to take food from the children and throw it to the dogs.'

[28]She replied, 'That's true, Lord, but even the dogs under the table are allowed to eat the scraps from the children's plates.'

[29]'Good answer!' he said. 'Now go home, for the demon has left your daughter.' [30]And when she arrived home, she found her little girl lying quietly in bed, and the demon was gone.

Jesus heals a deaf man

[31] Jesus left Tyre and went up to Sidon before going back to the Sea of Galilee and the region of the Ten Towns.[h] [32]A deaf man with a speech impediment was brought to him, and the people begged Jesus to lay his hands on the man to heal him.

[33]Jesus led him away from the crowd so they could be alone. He put his fingers into the man's ears. Then, spitting on his own fingers, he touched the man's tongue. [34]Looking up to heaven, he sighed and said, *'Ephphatha,'* which means, 'Be opened!' [35]Instantly the man could hear perfectly, and his tongue was freed so he could speak plainly!

[36]Jesus told the crowd not to tell anyone, but the more he told them not to, the more they spread the news. [37]They were completely amazed and said again and again, 'Everything he does is wonderful. He even makes the deaf to hear and gives speech to those who cannot speak.'

---

f   Greek *unclean.*

g   Greek *Let the children eat first.*

h   Greek *Decapolis*

Jesus feeds four thousand

8 About this time another large crowd had gathered, and the people ran out of food again. Jesus called his disciples and told them, [2]'I feel sorry for these people. They have been here with me for three days, and they have nothing left to eat. [3]If I send them home hungry, they will faint along the way. For some of them have come a long distance.'

[4]His disciples replied, 'How are we supposed to find enough food to feed them out here in the wilderness?'

[5] Jesus asked, 'How much bread do you have?'

'Seven loaves,' they replied.

[6]So Jesus told all the people to sit down on the ground. Then he took the seven loaves, thanked God for them, and broke them into pieces. He gave them to his disciples, who distributed the bread to the crowd. [7]A few small fish were found, too, so Jesus also blessed these and told the disciples to distribute them.

[8]They ate as much as they wanted. Afterwards, the disciples picked up seven large baskets of leftover food. [9]There were about 4,000 men in the crowd that day, and Jesus sent them home after they had eaten. [10]Immediately after this, he got into a boat with his disciples and crossed over to the region of Dalmanutha.

Pharisees demand a miraculous sign

[11]When the Pharisees heard that Jesus had arrived, they came and started to argue with him. Testing him, they demanded that he show them a miraculous sign from heaven to prove his authority.

[12]When he heard this, he sighed deeply in his spirit and said, 'Why do these people keep demanding a miraculous sign? I tell you the truth, I will not give this generation any such sign.' [13]So he got back into the boat and left them, and he crossed to the other side of the lake.

Yeast of the Pharisees and Herod

[14]But the disciples had forgotten to bring any food. They had only one loaf of bread with them in the boat. [15]As they were crossing the lake,

Jesus warned them, 'Watch out! Beware of the yeast of the Pharisees and of Herod.'

[16]At this they began to argue with each other because they hadn't brought any bread. [17]Jesus knew what they were saying, so he said, 'Why are you arguing about having no bread? Don't you know or understand even yet? Are your hearts too hard to take it in? [18]"You have eyes – can't you see? You have ears – can't you hear?"[i] Don't you remember anything at all? [19]When I fed the 5,000 with five loaves of bread, how many baskets of leftovers did you pick up afterwards?'

'Twelve,' they said.

[20]'And when I fed the 4,000 with seven loaves, how many large baskets of leftovers did you pick up?'

'Seven,' they said.

[21]'Don't you understand yet?' he asked them.

Jesus heals a blind man

[22]When they arrived at Bethsaida, some people brought a blind man to Jesus, and they begged him to touch the man and heal him. [23]Jesus took the blind man by the hand and led him out of the village. Then, spitting on the man's eyes, he laid his hands on him and asked, 'Can you see anything now?'

[24]The man looked around. 'Yes,' he said, 'I see people, but I can't see them very clearly. They look like trees walking around.'

[25]Then Jesus placed his hands on the man's eyes again, and his eyes were opened. His sight was completely restored, and he could see everything clearly. [26]Jesus sent him away, saying, 'Don't go back into the village on your way home.'

---

i   Jer 5:21.

Peter's declaration about Jesus

[27]Jesus and his disciples left Galilee and went up to the villages near Caesarea Philippi. As they were walking along, he asked them, 'Who do people say I am?'

[28]'Well,' they replied, 'some say John the Baptist, some say Elijah, and others say you are one of the other prophets.'

[29]Then he asked them, 'But who do you say I am?'

Peter replied, 'You are the Messiah.[a]'

[30]But Jesus warned them not to tell anyone about him.

Jesus predicts his death

[31]Then Jesus began to tell them that the Son of Man[b] must suffer many terrible things and be rejected by the elders, the leading priests, and the teachers of religious law. He would be killed, but three days later he would rise from the dead. [32]As he talked about this openly with his disciples, Peter took him aside and began to reprimand him for saying such things.[c]

[33]Jesus turned around and looked at his disciples, then reprimanded Peter. 'Get away from me, Satan!' he said. 'You are seeing things merely from a human point of view, not from God's.'

[34]Then, calling the crowd to join his disciples, he said, 'If any of you wants to be my follower, you must give up your own way, take up your cross, and follow me. [35]If you try to hang on to your life, you will lose it. But if you give up your life for my sake and for the sake of the Good News, you will save it. [36]And what do you benefit if you gain the whole world but lose your own soul?[d] [37]Is anything worth more than your soul? [38]If anyone is ashamed of me and my message in these adulterous and sinful days, the Son of Man will be ashamed

---

a Or *the Christ. Messiah* (a Hebrew term) and *Christ* (a Greek term) both mean 'anointed one'.

b 'Son of Man' is a title Jesus used for himself.

c Or *began to correct him.*

d Or *yourself?* also in 8:37.

of that person when he returns in the glory of his Father with the holy angels.'

9 Jesus went on to say, 'I tell you the truth, some standing here right now will not die before they see the Kingdom of God arrive in great power!'

The transfiguration

²Six days later Jesus took Peter, James, and John, and led them up a high mountain to be alone. As the men watched, Jesus' appearance was transformed, ³and his clothes became dazzling white, far whiter than any earthly bleach could ever make them. ⁴Then Elijah and Moses appeared and began talking with Jesus.

⁵Peter exclaimed, 'Rabbi, it's wonderful for us to be here! Let's make three shelters as memorials*ᵉ* – one for you, one for Moses, and one for Elijah.' ⁶He said this because he didn't really know what else to say, for they were all terrified.

⁷Then a cloud overshadowed them, and a voice from the cloud said, 'This is my dearly loved Son. Listen to him.' ⁸Suddenly, when they looked around, Moses and Elijah were gone, and they saw only Jesus with them.

⁹As they went back down the mountain, he told them not to tell anyone what they had seen until the Son of Man*ᶠ* had risen from the dead. ¹⁰So they kept it to themselves, but they often asked each other what he meant by 'rising from the dead'.

¹¹Then they asked him, 'Why do the teachers of religious law insist that Elijah must return before the Messiah comes?*ᵍ*'

¹²Jesus responded, 'Elijah is indeed coming first to get everything ready. Yet why do the Scriptures say that the Son of Man must suffer

---

e   Greek *three tabernacles.*

f   'Son of Man' is a title Jesus used for himself.

g   Greek *that Elijah must come first?*

greatly and be treated with utter contempt? [13]But I tell you, Elijah has already come, and they chose to abuse him, just as the Scriptures predicted.'

Jesus heals a demon-possessed boy

[14]When they returned to the other disciples, they saw a large crowd surrounding them, and some teachers of religious law were arguing with them. [15]When the crowd saw Jesus, they were overwhelmed with awe, and they ran to greet him.

[16]'What is all this arguing about?' Jesus asked.

[17]One of the men in the crowd spoke up and said, 'Teacher, I brought my son so you could heal him. He is possessed by an evil spirit that won't let him talk. [18]And whenever this spirit seizes him, it throws him violently to the ground. Then he foams at the mouth and grinds his teeth and becomes rigid.[h] So I asked your disciples to cast out the evil spirit, but they couldn't do it .'

[19] Jesus said to them,[i] 'You faithless people! How long must I be with you? How long must I put up with you? Bring the boy to me.'

[20]So they brought the boy. But when the evil spirit saw Jesus, it threw the child into a violent convulsion, and he fell to the ground, writhing and foaming at the mouth.

[21]'How long has this been happening?' Jesus asked the boy's father.

He replied, 'Since he was a little boy. [22]The spirit often throws him into the fire or into water, trying to kill him. Have mercy on us and help us, if you can.'

[23]'What do you mean, "If I can"?' Jesus asked. 'Anything is possible if a person believes.'

[24]The father instantly cried out, 'I do believe, but help me overcome my unbelief!'

---

h Or *becomes weak.*

i Or *said to his disciples.*

²⁵When Jesus saw that the crowd of onlookers was growing, he rebuked the evil*ʲ* spirit. 'Listen, you spirit that makes this boy unable to hear and speak,' he said. 'I command you to come out of this child and never enter him again!'

²⁶Then the spirit screamed and threw the boy into another violent convulsion and left him. The boy appeared to be dead. A murmur ran through the crowd as people said, 'He's dead.' ²⁷But Jesus took him by the hand and helped him to his feet, and he stood up.

²⁸Afterwards, when Jesus was alone in the house with his disciples, they asked him, 'Why couldn't we cast out that evil spirit?'

²⁹Jesus replied, 'This kind can be cast out only by prayer.*ᵏ*'

Jesus again predicts his death

³⁰Leaving that region, they travelled through Galilee. Jesus didn't want anyone to know he was there, ³¹for he wanted to spend more time with his disciples and teach them. He said to them, 'The Son of Man is going to be betrayed into the hands of his enemies. He will be killed, but three days later he will rise from the dead.' ³²They didn't understand what he was saying, however, and they were afraid to ask him what he meant.

The greatest in the kingdom

³³After they arrived at Capernaum and settled in a house, Jesus asked his disciples, 'What were you discussing out on the road?' ³⁴But they didn't answer, because they had been arguing about which of them was the greatest. ³⁵He sat down, called the twelve disciples over to him, and said, 'Whoever wants to be first must take last place and be the servant of everyone else.'

³⁶Then he put a little child among them. Taking the child in his arms, he said to them, ³⁷'Anyone who welcomes a little child like

---

j   Greek *unclean*.

k   Some manuscripts read *by prayer and fasting*.

this on my behalf*a* welcomes me, and anyone who welcomes me welcomes not only me but also my Father who sent me.'

Using the name of Jesus

³⁸John said to Jesus, 'Teacher, we saw someone using your name to cast out demons, but we told him to stop because he wasn't in our group.'

³⁹'Don't stop him!' Jesus said. 'No one who performs a miracle in my name will soon be able to speak evil of me. ⁴⁰Anyone who is not against us is for us. ⁴¹If anyone gives you even a cup of water because you belong to the Messiah, I tell you the truth, that person will surely be rewarded.

⁴²'But if you cause one of these little ones who trusts in me to fall into sin, it would be better for you to be thrown into the sea with a large millstone hung around your neck. ⁴³If your hand causes you to sin, cut it off. It's better to enter eternal life with only one hand than to go into the unquenchable fires of hell*b* with two hands.*c* ⁴⁵If your foot causes you to sin, cut it off. It's better to enter eternal life with only one foot than to be thrown into hell with two feet.*d* ⁴⁷And if your eye causes you to sin, gouge it out. It's better to enter the Kingdom of God with only one eye than to have two eyes and be thrown into hell, ⁴⁸"where the maggots never die and the fire never goes out".*e*

⁴⁹'For everyone will be tested with fire.*f* ⁵⁰Salt is good for seasoning. But if it loses its favour, how do you make it salty again? You must have the qualities of salt among yourselves and live in peace with each other.'

---

a Greek *in my name.*

b Greek *Gehenna;* also in 9:45, 47.

c Some manuscripts add verse 44, "*where the maggots never die and the fire never goes out*". See 9:48.

d Some manuscripts add verse 46, "*where the maggots never die and the fire never goes out*". See 9:48.

e Isa 66:24.

f Greek *salted with fire;* other manuscripts add *and every sacrifice will be salted with salt.*

Discussion about divorce and marriage

10Then Jesus left Capernaum and went down to the region of Judea and into the area east of the River Jordan. Once again crowds gathered around him, and as usual he was teaching them.

²Some Pharisees came and tried to trap him with this question: 'Should a man be allowed to divorce his wife?'

³ Jesus answered them with a question: 'What did Moses say in the law about divorce?'

⁴'Well, he permitted it,' they replied. 'He said a man can give his wife a written notice of divorce and send her away.'ᵍ

⁵But Jesus responded, 'He wrote this commandment only as a concession to your hard hearts. ⁶But "God made them male and female"ʰ from the beginning of creation. ⁷"This explains why a man leaves his father and mother and is joined to his wife,ⁱ ⁸and the two are united into one."ʲ Since they are no longer two but one, ⁹let no one split apart what God has joined together.'

¹⁰Later, when he was alone with his disciples in the house, they brought up the subject again. ¹¹He told them, 'Whoever divorces his wife and marries someone else commits adultery against her. ¹²And if a woman divorces her husband and marries someone else, she commits adultery.'

Jesus blesses the children

¹³One day some parents brought their children to Jesus so he could touch and bless them. But the disciples scolded the parents for bothering him.

¹⁴When Jesus saw what was happening, he was angry with his disciples. He said to them, 'Let the children come to me. Don't stop

---

g   See Deut 24:1.

h   Gen 1:27; 5:2.

i   Some manuscripts do not include *and is joined to his wife*.

j   Gen 2:24.

them! For the Kingdom of God belongs to those who are like these children. ¹⁵I tell you the truth, anyone who doesn't receive the Kingdom of God like a child will never enter it.' ¹⁶Then he took the children in his arms and placed his hands on their heads and blessed them.

The rich man

¹⁷As Jesus was starting out on his way to Jerusalem, a man came running up to him, knelt down, and asked, 'Good Teacher, what must I do to inherit eternal life?'

¹⁸'Why do you call me good?' Jesus asked. 'Only God is truly good. ¹⁹But to answer your question, you know the commandments: "You must not murder. You must not commit adultery. You must not steal. You must not testify falsely. You must not cheat anyone. Honour your father and mother."^k'

²⁰'Teacher,' the man replied, 'I've obeyed all these commandments since I was young.'

²¹Looking at the man, Jesus felt genuine love for him. 'There is still one thing you haven't done,' he told him. 'Go and sell all your possessions and give the money to the poor, and you will have treasure in heaven. Then come, follow me.'

²²At this the man's face fell, and he went away sad, for he had many possessions.

²³Jesus looked around and said to his disciples, 'How hard it is for the rich to enter the Kingdom of God!' ²⁴This amazed them. But Jesus said again, 'Dear children, it is very hard^l to enter the Kingdom of God. ²⁵In fact, it is easier for a camel to go through the eye of a needle than for a rich person to enter the Kingdom of God!'

²⁶The disciples were astounded. 'Then who in the world can be saved?' they asked.

---

k   Exod 20:12-16; Deut 5:16-20.

l   Some manuscripts read *very hard for those who trust in riches.*

²⁷Jesus looked at them intently and said, 'Humanly speaking, it is impossible. But not with God. Everything is possible with God.'

²⁸Then Peter began to speak up. 'We've given up everything to follow you,' he said.

²⁹'Yes,' Jesus replied, 'and I assure you that everyone who has given up house or brothers or sisters or mother or father or children or property, for my sake and for the Good News, ³⁰will receive now in return a hundred times as many houses, brothers, sisters, mothers, children, and property – along with persecution. And in the world to come that person will have eternal life. ³¹But many who are the greatest now will be least important then, and those who seem least important now will be the greatest then.'ᵐ'

Jesus again predicts his death

³²They were now on the way up to Jerusalem, and Jesus was walking ahead of them. The disciples were filled with awe, and the people following behind were overwhelmed with fear. Taking the twelve disciples aside, Jesus once more began to describe everything that was about to happen to him. ³³'Listen,' he said, 'we're going up to Jerusalem, where the Son of Manⁿ will be betrayed to the leading priests and the teachers of religious law. They will sentence him to die and hand him over to the Romans.ᵒ ³⁴They will mock him, spit on him, fog him with a whip, and kill him, but after three days he will rise again.'

Jesus teaches about serving others

³⁵Then James and John, the sons of Zebedee, came over and spoke to him. 'Teacher,' they said, 'we want you to do us a favour.'

³⁶'What is your request?' he asked.

---

m Greek *But many who are first will be last; and the last, first.*

n 'Son of Man' is a title Jesus used for himself.

o Greek *the Gentiles.*

[37]They replied, 'When you sit on your glorious throne, we want to sit in places of honour next to you, one on your right and the other on your left.'

[38]But Jesus said to them, 'You don't know what you are asking! Are you able to drink from the bitter cup of suffering I am about to drink? Are you able to be baptized with the baptism of suffering I must be baptized with?'

[39]'Oh yes,' they replied, 'we are able!'

Then Jesus told them, 'You will indeed drink from my bitter cup and be baptized with my baptism of suffering. [40]But I have no right to say who will sit on my right or my left. God has prepared those places for the ones he has chosen.'

[41]When the ten other disciples heard what James and John had asked, they were indignant. [42]So Jesus called them together and said, 'You know that the rulers in this world lord it over their people, and officials flaunt their authority over those under them. [43]But among you it will be different. Whoever wants to be a leader among you must be your servant, [44]and whoever wants to be first among you must be the slave of everyone else. [45]For even the Son of Man came not to be served but to serve others and to give his life as a ransom for many.'

Jesus heals blind Bartimaeus

[46]Then they reached Jericho, and as Jesus and his disciples left town, a large crowd followed him. A blind beggar named Bartimaeus (son of Timaeus) was sitting beside the road. [47]When Bartimaeus heard that Jesus of Nazareth was nearby, he began to shout, 'Jesus, Son of David, have mercy on me!'

[48]'Be quiet!' many of the people yelled at him.

But he only shouted louder, 'Son of David, have mercy on me!'

[49]When Jesus heard him, he stopped and said, 'Tell him to come here.'

So they called the blind man. 'Cheer up,' they said. 'Come on, he's calling you!' [50]Bartimaeus threw aside his coat, jumped up, and came to Jesus.

[51]'What do you want me to do for you?' Jesus asked.

'My Rabbi,[a]' the blind man said, 'I want to see!'

[52]And Jesus said to him, 'Go, for your faith has healed you.' Instantly the man could see, and he followed Jesus down the road.[b]

Jesus' triumphant entry

11 As Jesus and his disciples approached Jerusalem, they came to the towns of Bethphage and Bethany on the Mount of Olives. Jesus sent two of them on ahead. [2]'Go into that village over there,' he told them. 'As soon as you enter it, you will see a young donkey tied there that no one has ever ridden. Untie it and bring it here. [3]If anyone asks, "What are you doing?" just say, "The Lord needs it and will return it soon."'

[4]The two disciples left and found the colt standing in the street, tied outside the front door. [5]As they were untying it, some bystanders demanded, 'What are you doing, untying that colt?' [6]They said what Jesus had told them to say, and they were permitted to take it. [7]Then they brought the colt to Jesus and threw their garments over it, and he sat on it.

[8]Many in the crowd spread their garments on the road ahead of him, and others spread leafy branches they had cut in the fields. [9]Jesus was in the centre of the procession, and the people all around him were shouting,

'Praise God![c]
  Blessings on the one who comes in the name of the
    Lord!
[10] Blessings on the coming Kingdom of our ancestor David!
  Praise God in highest heaven!'[d]

---

a   Greek uses the Hebrew term *Rabboni*.

b   Or *on the way*.

c   Greek *Hosanna*, an exclamation of praise that literally means 'save now'; also in 11:10.

d   Pss 118:25-26; 148:1.

¹¹So Jesus came to Jerusalem and went into the Temple. After looking around carefully at everything, he left because it was late in the afternoon. Then he returned to Bethany with the twelve disciples.

Jesus curses the fig tree

¹²The next morning as they were leaving Bethany, Jesus was hungry. ¹³He noticed a fig tree in full leaf a little way of, so he went over to see if he could find any figs. But there were only leaves because it was too early in the season for fruit. ¹⁴Then Jesus said to the tree, 'May no one ever eat your fruit again!' And the disciples heard him say it.

Jesus clears the Temple

¹⁵When they arrived back in Jerusalem, Jesus entered the Temple and began to drive out the people buying and selling animals for sacrifices. He knocked over the tables of the money changers and the chairs of those selling doves, ¹⁶and he stopped everyone from using the Temple as a market-place.*e* ¹⁷He said to them, 'The Scriptures declare, "My Temple will be called a house of prayer for all nations," but you have turned it into a den of thieves.'*f*

¹⁸When the leading priests and teachers of religious law heard what Jesus had done, they began planning how to kill him. But they were afraid of him because the people were so amazed at his teaching.

¹⁹That evening Jesus and the disciples left*g* the city.

²⁰The next morning as they passed by the fig tree he had cursed, the disciples noticed it had withered from the roots up. ²¹Peter remembered what Jesus had said to the tree on the previous day and exclaimed, 'Look, Rabbi! The fig tree you cursed has withered and died!'

---

e   Or *from carrying merchandise through the Temple.*

f   Isa 56:7; Jer 7:11.

g   Greek *they left;* other manuscripts read *he left.*

[22]Then Jesus said to the disciples, 'Have faith in God. [23]I tell you the truth, you can say to this mountain, "May you be lifted up and thrown into the sea," and it will happen. But you must really believe it will happen and have no doubt in your heart. [24]I tell you, you can pray for anything, and if you believe that you've received it, it will be yours. [25]But when you are praying, first forgive anyone you are holding a grudge against, so that your Father in heaven will forgive your sins, too.[h]'

The authority of Jesus challenged

[27]Again they entered Jerusalem. As Jesus was walking through the Temple area, the leading priests, the teachers of religious law, and the elders came up to him. [28]They demanded, 'By what authority are you doing all these things? Who gave you the right to do them?'

[29]'I'll tell you by what authority I do these things if you answer one question,' Jesus replied. [30]'Did John's authority to baptize come from heaven, or was it merely human? Answer me!'

[31]They talked it over among themselves. 'If we say it was from heaven, he will ask why we didn't believe John. [32]But do we dare say it was merely human?' For they were afraid of what the people would do, because everyone believed that John was a prophet. [33]So they finally replied, 'We don't know.'

And Jesus responded, 'Then I won't tell you by what authority I do these things.'

Parable of the evil farmers

12 Then Jesus began teaching them with stories: 'A man planted a vineyard. He built a wall around it, dug a pit for pressing out the grape juice, and built a lookout tower. Then he leased the vineyard to tenant farmers and moved to another country. [2]At the time of the grape harvest, he sent one of his servants to collect his share

---

h   Some manuscripts add verse 26, *But if you refuse to forgive, your Father in heaven will not forgive your sins.* Compare Matt 6:15.

of the crop. [3]But the farmers grabbed the servant, beat him up, and sent him back empty-handed. [4]The owner then sent another servant, but they insulted him and beat him over the head. [5]The next servant he sent was killed. Others he sent were either beaten or killed, [6]until there was only one left – his son whom he loved dearly. The owner finally sent him, thinking, "Surely they will respect my son."

[7]'But the tenant farmers said to one another, "Here comes the heir to this estate. Let's kill him and get the estate for ourselves!" [8]So they grabbed him and murdered him and threw his body out of the vineyard.

[9]'What do you suppose the owner of the vineyard will do?' Jesus asked. 'I'll tell you – he will come and kill those farmers and lease the vineyard to others. [10]Didn't you ever read this in the Scriptures?

"The stone that the builders rejected
    has now become the cornerstone.
[11]This is the Lord's doing,
    and it is wonderful to see."[a]'

[12]The religious leaders[b] wanted to arrest Jesus because they realized he was telling the story against them – they were the wicked farmers. But they were afraid of the crowd, so they left him and went away.

Taxes for Caesar

[13]Later the leaders sent some Pharisees and supporters of Herod to trap Jesus into saying something for which he could be arrested. [14]'Teacher,' they said, 'we know how honest you are. You are impartial and don't have favourites. You teach the way of God truthfully. Now tell us – is it right to pay taxes to Caesar or not? [15]Should we pay them, or shouldn't we?'

---

a   Ps 118:22-23.

b   Greek *They*.

Jesus saw through their hypocrisy and said, 'Why are you trying to trap me? Show me a Roman coin,[c] and I'll tell you.' [16]When they handed it to him, he asked, 'Whose picture and title are stamped on it?'

'Caesar's,' they replied.

[17]'Well, then,' Jesus said, 'give to Caesar what belongs to Caesar, and give to God what belongs to God.'

His reply completely amazed them.

Discussion about resurrection

[18]Then Jesus was approached by some Sadducees – religious leaders who say there is no resurrection from the dead. They posed this question: [19]'Teacher, Moses gave us a law that if a man dies, leaving a wife without children, his brother should marry the widow and have a child who will carry on the brother's name.[d] [20]Well, suppose there were seven brothers. The oldest one married and then died without children. [21]So the second brother married the widow, but he also died without children. Then the third brother married her. [22]This continued with all seven of them, and still there were no children. Last of all, the woman also died. [23]So tell us, whose wife will she be in the resurrection? For all seven were married to her.'

[24]Jesus replied, 'Your mistake is that you don't know the Scriptures, and you don't know the power of God. [25]For when the dead rise, they will neither marry nor be given in marriage. In this respect they will be like the angels in heaven.

[26]'But now, as to whether the dead will be raised – haven't you ever read about this in the writings of Moses, in the story of the burning bush? Long after Abraham, Isaac, and Jacob had died, God said to Moses,[e] "I am the God of Abraham, the God of Isaac, and the God of

---

c   Greek *a denarius.*

d   See Deut 25:5-6.

e   Greek *in the story of the bush? God said to him.*

Jacob." [f] [27]So he is the God of the living, not the dead. You have made a serious error.'

The most important commandment

[28]One of the teachers of religious law was standing there listening to the debate. He realized that Jesus had answered well, so he asked, 'Of all the commandments, which is the most important?'

[29]Jesus replied, 'The most important commandment is this: "Listen, O Israel! The Lord our God is the one and only Lord. [30]And you must love the Lord your God with all your heart, all your soul, all your mind, and all your strength."[g] [31]The second is equally important: "Love your neighbour as yourself."[h] No other commandment is greater than these.'

[32]The teacher of religious law replied, 'Well said, Teacher. You have spoken the truth by saying that there is only one God and no other. [33]And I know it is important to love him with all my heart and all my understanding and all my strength, and to love my neighbour as myself. This is more important than to offer all of the burnt offerings and sacrifices required in the law.'

[34]Realizing how much the man understood, Jesus said to him, 'You are not far from the Kingdom of God.' And after that, no one dared to ask him any more questions.

Whose son is the Messiah?

[35]Later, as Jesus was teaching the people in the Temple, he asked, 'Why do the teachers of religious law claim that the Messiah is the son of David? [36]For David himself, speaking under the inspiration of the Holy Spirit, said,

---

[f]   Exod 3:6.

[g]   Deut 6:4-5.

[h]   Lev 19:18.

"The LORD said to my Lord,
Sit in the place of honour at my right hand
until I humble your enemies beneath your feet."[i]

[37]Since David himself called the Messiah "my Lord", how can the Messiah be his son?' The large crowd listened to him with great delight.

[38]Jesus also taught: 'Beware of these teachers of religious law! For they like to parade around in flowing robes and receive respectful greetings as they walk in the market-places. [39]And how they love the seats of honour in the synagogues and the head table at banquets. [40]Yet they shamelessly cheat widows out of their property and then pretend to be pious by making long prayers in public. Because of this, they will be more severely punished.'

The widow's offering

[41]Jesus sat down near the collection box in the Temple and watched as the crowds dropped in their money. Many rich people put in large amounts. [42]Then a poor widow came and dropped in two small coins.[j]

[43]Jesus called his disciples to him and said, 'I tell you the truth, this poor widow has given more than all the others who are making contributions. [44]For they gave a tiny part of their surplus, but she, poor as she is, has given everything she had to live on.'

Jesus speaks about the future

13 As Jesus was leaving the Temple that day, one of his disciples said, 'Teacher, look at these magnificent buildings! Look at the impressive stones in the walls.'

---

i   Ps 110:1.
j   Greek *two lepta, which is a kodrantes* [i.e., a quadrans].

²Jesus replied, 'Yes, look at these great buildings. But they will be completely demolished. Not one stone will be left on top of another!'

³Later, Jesus sat on the Mount of Olives across the valley from the Temple. Peter, James, John, and Andrew came to him privately and asked him, ⁴"Tell us, when will all this happen? What sign will show us that these things are about to be fulfilled?'

⁵Jesus replied, 'Don't let anyone mislead you, ⁶for many will come in my name, claiming, "I am the Messiah."ᵃ They will deceive many. ⁷And you will hear of wars and threats of wars, but don't panic. Yes, these things must take place, but the end won't follow immediately. ⁸Nation will go to war against nation, and kingdom against kingdom. There will be earthquakes in many parts of the world, as well as famines. But this is only the first of the birth pains, with more to come.

⁹'When these things begin to happen, watch out! You will be handed over to the local councils and beaten in the synagogues. You will stand trial before governors and kings because you are my followers. But this will be your opportunity to tell them about me.ᵇ ¹⁰For the Good News must first be preached to all nations.ᶜ ¹¹But when you are arrested and stand trial, don't worry in advance about what to say. Just say what God tells you at that time, for it is not you who will be speaking, but the Holy Spirit.

¹²'A brother will betray his brother to death, a father will betray his own child, and children will rebel against their parents and cause them to be killed. ¹³And every one will hate you because you are my followers.ᵈ But the one who endures to the end will be saved.

¹⁴'The day is coming when you will see the sacrilegious object that causes desecrationᵉ standing where heᶠ should not be.' (Reader, pay

---

a   Greek *claiming, "I am"*.

b   Or *But this will be your testimony against them.*

c   Or *all peoples.*

d   Greek *on account of my name.*

e   Greek *the abomination of desolation.* See Dan 9:27; 11:31; 12:11.

f   Or *it.*

attention!) 'Then those in Judea must flee to the hills. [15]A person out on the deck of a roof must not go down into the house to pack. [16]A person out in the field must not return even to get a coat. [17]How terrible it will be for pregnant women and for nursing mothers in those days. [18]And pray that your flight will not be in winter. [19]For there will be greater anguish in those days than at any time since God created the world. And it will never be so great again. [20]In fact, unless the Lord shortens that time of calamity, not a single person will survive. But for the sake of his chosen ones he has shortened those days.

[21]'Then if anyone tells you, "Look, here is the Messiah," or "There he is," don't believe it. [22]For false messiahs and false prophets will rise up and perform signs and wonders so as to deceive, if possible, even God's chosen ones. [23]Watch out! I have warned you about this ahead of time!

[24]'At that time, after the anguish of those days,

the sun will be darkened,
    the moon will give no light,
[25]the stars will fall from the sky,
    and the powers in the heavens will be shaken.[g]

[26]Then every one will see the Son of Man[h] coming on the clouds with great power and glory.[i] [27]And he will send out his angels to gather his chosen ones from all over the world[j] – from the farthest ends of the earth and heaven.

[28]'Now learn a lesson from the fig tree. When its branches bud and its leaves begin to sprout, you know that summer is near. [29]In the same way, when you see all these things taking place, you can

---

g See Isa 13:10; 34:4; Joel 2:10.

h 'Son of Man' is a title Jesus used for himself.

i See Dan 7:13.

j Greek *from the four winds.*

know that his return is very near, right at the door. ³⁰I tell you the truth, this generation*ᵏ* will not pass from the scene before all these things take place. ³¹Heaven and earth will disappear, but my words will never disappear.

³²'However, no one knows the day or hour when these things will happen, not even the angels in heaven or the Son himself. Only the Father knows. ³³And since you don't know when that time will come, be on guard! Stay alert!*ˡ*

³⁴'The coming of the Son of Man can be illustrated by the story of a man going on a long trip. When he left home, he gave each of his slaves instructions about the work they were to do, and he told the gate keeper to watch for his return. ³⁵You, too, must keep watch! For you don't know when the master of the household will return – in the evening, at midnight, before dawn, or at daybreak. ³⁶Don't let him find you sleeping when he arrives without warning. ³⁷I say to you what I say to every one: Watch for him!'

Jesus anointed at Bethany

14 It was now two days before Passover and the Festival of Unleavened Bread. The leading priests and the teachers of religious law were still looking for an opportunity to capture Jesus secretly and kill him. ²'But not during the Passover celebration,' they agreed, 'or the people may riot.'

³Meanwhile, Jesus was in Bethany at the home of Simon, a man who had previously had leprosy. While he was eating,*ᵐ* a woman came in with a beautiful alabaster jar of expensive perfume made from essence of nard. She broke open the jar and poured the perfume over his head.

---

k Or *this age*, or *this nation*.

l Some manuscripts add *and pray*.

m Or *reclining*.

[4]Some of those at the table were indignant. 'Why waste such expensive perfume?' they asked. [5]'It could have been sold for a year's wages[n] and the money given to the poor!' So they scolded her harshly.

[6]But Jesus replied, 'Leave her alone. Why criticize her for doing such a good thing to me? [7]You will always have the poor among you, and you can help them whenever you want to. But you will not always have me. [8]She has done what she could and has anointed my body for burial ahead of time. [9]I tell you the truth, wherever the Good News is preached throughout the world, this woman's deed will be remembered and discussed.'

Judas agrees to betray Jesus

[10]Then Judas Iscariot, one of the twelve disciples, went to the leading priests to arrange to betray Jesus to them. [11]They were delighted when they heard why he had come, and they promised to give him money. So he began looking for an opportunity to betray Jesus.

The Last Supper

[12]On the first day of the Festival of Unleavened Bread, when the Passover lamb is sacrificed, Jesus' disciples asked him, 'Where do you want us to go to prepare the Passover meal for you?'

[13]So Jesus sent two of them into Jerusalem with these instructions: 'As you go into the city, a man carrying a jug of water will meet you. Follow him. [14]At the house he enters, say to the owner, "The Teacher asks: Where is the guest room where I can eat the Passover meal with my disciples?" [15]He will take you upstairs to a large room that is already set up. That is where you should prepare our meal.' [16]So the two disciples went into the city and found everything just as Jesus had said, and they prepared the Passover meal there.

---

n   Greek *for 300 denarii*. A denarius was equivalent to a labourer's full day's wage.

[17]In the evening Jesus arrived with the Twelve. [18]As they were at the table[a] eating, Jesus said, 'I tell you the truth, one of you eating with me here will betray me.'

[19]Greatly distressed, each one asked in turn, 'Am I the one?'

[20]He replied, 'It is one of you twelve who is eating from this bowl with me. [21]For the Son of Man[b] must die, as the Scriptures declared long ago. But how terrible it will be for the one who betrays him. It would be far better for that man if he had never been born!'

[22]As they were eating, Jesus took some bread and blessed it. Then he broke it in pieces and gave it to the disciples, saying, 'Take it, for this is my body.'

[23]And he took a cup of wine and gave thanks to God for it. He gave it to them, and they all drank from it. [24]And he said to them, 'This is my blood, which confirms the covenant[c] between God and his people. It is poured out as a sacrifice for many. [25]I tell you the truth, I will not drink wine again until the day I drink it new in the Kingdom of God.'

[26]Then they sang a hymn and went out to the Mount of Olives.

Jesus predicts Peter's denial

[27]On the way, Jesus told them, 'All of you will desert me. For the Scriptures say,

"God will strike[d] the Shepherd, and the sheep will be scattered."

[28]But after I am raised from the dead, I will go ahead of you to Galilee and meet you there.'

[29]Peter said to him, 'Even if everyone else deserts you, I never will.'

---

a   Or *As they reclined.*

b   'Son of Man' is a title Jesus used for himself.

c   Some manuscripts read *the new covenant.*

d   Greek *I will strike.* Zech 13:7.

[30]Jesus replied, 'I tell you the truth, Peter – this very night, before the cock crows twice, you will deny three times that you even know me.'

[31]'No!' Peter declared emphatically. 'Even if I have to die with you, I will never deny you!' And all the others vowed the same.

Jesus prays in Gethsemane

[32]They went to the olive grove called Gethsemane, and Jesus said, 'Sit here while I go and pray.' [33]He took Peter, James, and John with him, and he became deeply troubled and distressed. [34]He told them, 'My soul is crushed with grief to the point of death. Stay here and keep watch with me.'

[35]He went on a little farther and fell to the ground. He prayed that, if it were possible, the awful hour awaiting him might pass him by. [36]'Abba, Father,'[e] he cried out, 'everything is possible for you. Please take this cup of suffering away from me. Yet I want your will to be done, not mine.'

[37]Then he returned and found the disciples asleep. He said to Peter, 'Simon, are you asleep? Couldn't you watch with me for even one hour? [38]Keep watch and pray, so that you will not give in to temptation. For the spirit is willing, but the body is weak.'

[39]Then Jesus left them again and prayed the same prayer as before. [40]When he returned to them again, he found them sleeping, for they couldn't keep their eyes open. And they didn't know what to say.

[41]When he returned to them the third time, he said, 'Go ahead and sleep. Have your rest. But no – the time has come. The Son of Man is betrayed into the hands of sinners. [42]Up, let's be going. Look, my betrayer is here!'

---

e   *Abba* is an Aramaic term for 'father'.

Jesus is betrayed and arrested

[43]And immediately, even as Jesus said this, Judas, one of the twelve disciples, arrived with a crowd of men armed with swords and clubs. They had been sent by the leading priests, the teachers of religious law, and the elders. [44]The traitor, Judas, had given them a prearranged signal: 'You will know which one to arrest when I greet him with a kiss. Then you can take him away under guard.' [45]As soon as they arrived, Judas walked up to Jesus. 'Rabbi!' he exclaimed, and gave him the kiss.

[46]Then the others grabbed Jesus and arrested him. [47]But one of the men with Jesus pulled out his sword and struck the high priest's slave, slashing of his ear.

[48]Jesus asked them, 'Am I some dangerous revolutionary, that you come with swords and clubs to arrest me? [49]Why didn't you arrest me in the Temple? I was there among you teaching every day. But these things are happening to fulfil what the Scriptures say about me.'

[50]Then all his disciples deserted him and ran away. [51]One young man following behind was clothed only in a long linen shirt. When the mob tried to grab him, [52]he slipped out of his shirt and ran away naked.

Jesus before the council

[53]They took Jesus to the high priest's home where the leading priests, the elders, and the teachers of religious law had gathered. [54]Meanwhile, Peter followed him at a distance and went right into the high priest's courtyard. There he sat with the guards, warming himself by the fire.

[55]Inside, the leading priests and the entire high council[f] were trying to find evidence against Jesus, so they could put him to death.

---

f Greek the Sanhedrin.

But they couldn't find any. [56]Many false witnesses spoke against him, but they contradicted each other. [57]Finally, some men stood up and gave this false testimony: [58]'We heard him say, "I will destroy this Temple made with human hands, and in three days I will build another, made without human hands."' [59]But even then they didn't get their stories straight!

[60]Then the high priest stood up before the others and asked Jesus, 'Well, aren't you going to answer these charges? What do you have to say for yourself?' [61]But Jesus was silent and made no reply. Then the high priest asked him, 'Are you the Messiah, the Son of the Blessed One?'

[62]Jesus said, 'I Am.[g] And you will see the Son of Man seated in the place of power at God's right hand[h] and coming on the clouds of heaven.[i]

[63]Then the high priest tore his clothing to show his horror and said, 'Why do we need other witnesses? [64]You have all heard his blasphemy. What is your verdict?'

'Guilty!' they all cried. 'He deserves to die!'

[65]Then some of them began to spit at him, and they blindfolded him and beat him with their fists. 'Prophesy to us,' they jeered. And the guards slapped him as they took him away.

Peter denies Jesus

[66]Meanwhile, Peter was in the courtyard below. One of the servant girls who worked for the high priest came by [67]and noticed Peter warming himself at the fire. She looked at him closely and said, 'You were one of those with Jesus of Nazareth.[j] [68]But Peter denied it.

---

g   Or *The "I am" is here*; or *I am the Lord*. See Exod 3:14.

h   Greek *seated at the right hand of the power*. See Ps 110:1.

i   See Dan 7:13.

j   Or *Jesus the Nazarene*.

'I don't know what you're talking about,' he said, and he went out into the courtyard. Just then, a cock crowed.[a]

[69]When the servant girl saw him standing there, she began telling the others, 'This man is definitely one of them!' [70]But Peter denied it again.

A little later some of the other bystanders confronted Peter and said, 'You must be one of them, because you are a Galilean.'

[71]Peter swore, 'A curse on me if I'm lying – I don't know this man you're talking about!' [72]And immediately the cock crowed the second time.

Suddenly, Jesus' words flashed through Peter's mind: 'Before the cock crows twice, you will deny three times that you even know me.' And he broke down and wept.

Jesus' trial before Pilate

15 Very early in the morning the leading priests, the elders, and the teachers of religious law – the entire high council[b] – met to discuss their next step. They bound Jesus, led him away, and took him to Pilate, the Roman governor.

[2]Pilate asked Jesus, 'Are you the king of the Jews?'

Jesus replied, 'You have said it.'

[3]Then the leading priests kept accusing him of many crimes, [4]and Pilate asked him, 'Aren't you going to answer them? What about all these charges they are bringing against you?' [5]But Jesus said nothing, much to Pilate's surprise.

[6]Now it was the governor's custom each year during the Passover celebration to release one prisoner – anyone the people requested. [7]One of the prisoners at that time was Barabbas, a revolutionary who had committed murder in an uprising. [8]The crowd went to Pilate and asked him to release a prisoner as usual.

---

a Some manuscripts do not include *Just then, a cock crowed.*

b Greek *the Sanhedrin;* also in 15:43.

[9]'Would you like me to release to you this "King of the Jews'?' Pilate asked. [10](For he realized by now that the leading priests had arrested Jesus out of envy.) [11]But at this point the leading priests stirred up the crowd to demand the release of Barabbas instead of Jesus. [12]Pilate asked them, 'Then what should I do with this man you call the king of the Jews?'

[13]They shouted back, 'Crucify him!'

[14]'Why?' Pilate demanded. 'What crime has he committed?'

But the mob roared even louder, 'Crucify him!'

[15]So to pacify the crowd, Pilate released Barabbas to them. He ordered Jesus to be fogged with a lead-tipped whip, then turned him over to the Roman soldiers to be crucified.

The soldiers mock Jesus

[16]The soldiers took Jesus into the courtyard of the governor's head quarters (called the Praetorium) and called out the entire regiment. [17]They dressed him in a purple robe, and they wove thorn branches into a crown and put it on his head. [18]Then they saluted him and taunted, 'Hail! King of the Jews!' [19]And they struck him on the head with a reed stick, spat on him, and dropped to their knees in mock worship. [20]When they were finally tired of mocking him, they took of the purple robe and put his own clothes on him again. Then they led him away to be crucified.

The crucifixion

[21]A passerby named Simon, who was from Cyrene,[c] was coming in from the countryside just then, and the soldiers forced him to carry Jesus' cross. (Simon was the father of Alexander and Rufus.) [22]And they brought Jesus to a place called Golgotha (which means 'Place of the Skull'). [23]They offered him wine drugged with myrrh, but he refused it.

---

c *Cyrene* was a city in northern Africa.

[24]Then the soldiers nailed him to the cross. They divided his clothes and threw dice[d] to decide who would get each piece. [25]It was nine o'clock in the morning when they crucified him. [26]A sign announced the charge against him. It read, 'The King of the Jews'. [27]Two revolutionaries[e] were crucified with him, one on his right and one on his left.[f]

[29]The people passing by shouted abuse, shaking their heads in mockery. 'Ha! Look at you now!' they yelled at him. 'You said you were going to destroy the Temple and rebuild it in three days. [30]Well then, save yourself and come down from the cross!'

[31]The leading priests and teachers of religious law also mocked Jesus. 'He saved others,' they scoffed, 'but he can't save himself! [32]Let this Messiah, this King of Israel, come down from the cross so we can see it and believe him!' Even the men who were crucified with Jesus ridiculed him.

The death of Jesus

[33]At midday, darkness fell across the whole land until three o'clock. [34]Then at three o'clock Jesus called out with a loud voice, *'Eloi, Eloi, lema sabachthani?'* which means 'My God, my God, why have you abandoned me?'[g]

[35]Some of the bystanders misunderstood and thought he was calling for the prophet Elijah. [36]One of them ran and filled a sponge with sour wine, holding it up to him on a reed stick so he could drink. 'Wait!' he said. 'Let's see whether Elijah comes to take him down!'

[37]Then Jesus uttered another loud cry and breathed his last. [38]And the curtain in the sanctuary of the Temple was torn in two, from top to bottom.

---

d   Greek *cast lots.* See Ps 22:18.

e   Or *Two criminals.*

f   Some manuscripts add verse 28, *And the Scripture was fulfilled that said, 'He was counted among those who were rebels.'* See Isa 53:12; also compare Luke 22:37.

g   Ps 22:1.

[39]When the Roman officer[h] who stood facing him[i] saw how he had died, he exclaimed, 'This man truly was the Son of God!'

[40]Some women were there, watching from a distance, including Mary Magdalene, Mary (the mother of James the younger and of Joseph[j]), and Salome. [41]They had been followers of Jesus and had cared for him while he was in Galilee. Many other women who had come with him to Jerusalem were also there.

The burial of Jesus

[42]This all happened on Friday, the day of preparation,[k] the day before the Sabbath. As evening approached, [43]Joseph of Arimathea took a risk and went to Pilate and asked for Jesus' body. (Joseph was an honoured member of the high council, and he was waiting for the Kingdom of God to come.) [44]Pilate couldn't believe that Jesus was already dead, so he called for the Roman officer and asked if he had died yet. [45]The officer confirmed that Jesus was dead, so Pilate told Joseph he could have the body. [46]Joseph bought a long sheet of linen cloth. Then he took Jesus' body down from the cross, wrapped it in the cloth, and laid it in a tomb that had been carved out of the rock. Then he rolled a stone in front of the entrance. [47]Mary Magdalene and Mary the mother of Joseph saw where Jesus' body was laid.

The resurrection

16 Saturday evening, when the Sabbath ended, Mary Magdalene, Mary the mother of James, and Salome went out and purchased burial spices so they could anoint Jesus' body. [2]Very early on Sunday

---

h   Greek *the centurion;* similarly in 15:44, 45.

i   Some manuscripts add *heard his cry and.*

j   Greek *Joses;* also in 15:47. See Matt 27:56.

k   Greek *It was the day of preparation.*

morning,[a] just at sunrise, they went to the tomb. ³On the way they were asking each other, 'Who will roll away the stone for us from the entrance to the tomb?' ⁴But as they arrived, they looked up and saw that the stone, which was very large, had already been rolled aside.

⁵When they entered the tomb, they saw a young man clothed in a white robe sitting on the right side. The women were shocked, ⁶but the angel said, 'Don't be alarmed. You are looking for Jesus of Nazareth,[b] who was crucified. He isn't here! He is risen from the dead! Look, this is where they laid his body. ⁷Now go and tell his disciples, including Peter, that Jesus is going ahead of you to Galilee. You will see him there, just as he told you before he died.'

⁸The women fed from the tomb, trembling and bewildered, and they said nothing to anyone because they were too frightened.[c]

*[The most ancient manuscripts of Mark conclude
with verse 16:8. Later manuscripts add one or
both of the following endings.]*

[Shorter Ending of Mark]

Then they briefly reported all this to Peter and his companions. Afterwards Jesus himself sent them out from east to west with the sacred and unfailing message of salvation that gives eternal life. Amen.

[Longer Ending of Mark]

⁹After Jesus rose from the dead early on Sunday morning, the first person who saw him was Mary Magdalene, the woman from whom

---

a   Greek *on the first day of the week;* also in 16:9.

b   Or *Jesus the Nazarene.*

c   The most reliable early manuscripts of the Gospel of Mark end at verse 8. Other manuscripts include various endings to the Gospel. A few include both the 'shorter ending' and the 'longer ending'. The majority of manuscripts include the 'longer ending' immediately after verse 8.

he had cast out seven demons. [10]She went to the disciples, who were grieving and weeping, and told them what had happened. [11]But when she told them that Jesus was alive and she had seen him, they didn't believe her.

[12]Afterwards he appeared in a different form to two of his followers who were walking from Jerusalem into the country. [13]They rushed back to tell the others, but no one believed them.

[14]Still later he appeared to the eleven disciples as they were eating together. He rebuked them for their stubborn unbelief because they refused to believe those who had seen him after he had been raised from the dead.[d]

[15]And then he told them, 'Go into all the world and preach the Good News to everyone. [16]Anyone who believes and is baptized will be saved. But anyone who refuses to believe will be condemned. [17]These miraculous signs will accompany those who believe: They will cast out demons in my name, and they will speak in new languages.[e] [18]They will be able to handle snakes with safety, and if they drink anything poisonous, it won't hurt them. They will be able to place their hands on the sick, and they will be healed.'

[19]When the Lord Jesus had finished talking with them, he was taken up into heaven and sat down in the place of honour at God's right hand. [20]And the disciples went everywhere and preached, and the Lord worked through them, confirming what they said by many miraculous signs.

---

d Some early manuscripts add: *And they excused themselves, saying, 'This age of law-lessness and unbelief is under Satan, who does not permit God's truth and power to conquer the evil [unclean] spirits. Therefore, reveal your justice now.' This is what they said to Christ. And Christ replied to them, 'The period of years of Satan's power has been fulfilled, but other dreadful things will happen soon. And I was handed over to death for those who have sinned, so that they may return to the truth and sin no more, and so they may inherit the spiritual, incorruptible, and righteous glory in heaven.'*

e Or *new tongues;* some manuscripts do not include *new.*

Notes

1 C. S. Lewis, *Surprised by Joy: The Shape of My Early Life* (London: Geoffrey Bles, 1955), chapter 14. *Surprised By Joy* by C. S. Lewis © copyright C. S. Lewis Pte Ltd 1955. Extract used with permission.
2 'Worship', Oxford English Dictionary, <https://www.lexico.com/definition/worship>.
3 N. T. Wright, *Simply Christian: Why Christianity Makes Sense* (London: SPCK, 2011), p. 123.
4 'Eternal', Oxford English Dictionary, <https://www.lexico.com/definition/eternal>.
5 Charlene Laino, 'Going to Church May Improve Mental Health', WebMD, 26 May 2005, <www.webmd.com/mental-health/news/20050526/going-church-may-improve-mental-health>.
6 Christopher G, Ellison, Terrence D. Hill and Reed T. DeAngelis, 'Religious involvement as a social determinant of sleep: an initial review and conceptual model', *Sleep Health* (Journal of the National Sleep Foundation), 2018.

WE HAVE A VISION OF A WORLD IN WHICH EVERYONE IS TRANSFORMED BY CHRISTIAN KNOWLEDGE

As well as being an award-winning publisher, SPCK is the oldest Anglican mission agency in the world.

Our mission is to lead the way in creating books and resources that help everyone to make sense of faith.

Will you partner with us to put good books into the hands of prisoners, great assemblies in front of schoolchildren and reach out to people who have not yet been touched by the Christian faith?

To donate, please visit www.spckpublishing.co.uk/donate or call our friendly fundraising team on 020 7592 3900.

An easy way to get to know the Bible

'For those who've been putting aside two years in later life to read the Bible from cover to cover, the good news is: the most important bits are here.' Jeremy Vine, BBC Radio 2

The Bible is full of dramatic stories that have made it the world's bestselling book. But whoever has time to read it all from cover to cover? Now here's a way of getting to know the Bible without having to read every chapter and verse.

No summary, no paraphrase, no commentary: just the Bible's own story in the Bible's own words.

'What an amazing concept! This compelling, concise, slimmed-down Scripture is a must for anyone who finds those sixty-six books a tad daunting.'
Paul Kerensa, comedian and script writer

'A great introduction to the main stories in the Bible and it helps you to see how they fit together. It would be great to give as a gift.'
Five-star review on Amazon

The One Hour Bible
978 0 281 07964 3 • £4.99